T0270512

RUBATO EXPRESSO

DEFEATING DENGUE

A MULTISTAKEHOLDER
APPROACH TO PROBLEM SOLVING

R. EDWARD FREEMAN
AND ANDREW SELL

Columbia University Press   *New York*

Columbia University Press
Publishers Since 1893
New York   Chichester, West Sussex
cup.columbia.edu

Copyright © 2024 R. Edward Freeman and Andrew Sell
All rights reserved

Library of Congress Cataloging-in-Publication Data
Names: Freeman, R. Edward, 1951– author. | Sell, Andrew, author.
Title: Defeating dengue : a multistakeholder approach to problem
solving / R. Edward Freeman and Andrew Sell.
Description: New York : Columbia University Press, [2024] |
Includes bibliographical references and index.
Identifiers: LCCN 2024008881 | ISBN 9780231215565 (hardback) |
ISBN 9780231560856 (ebook)
Subjects: LCSH: Dengue—Indonesia. | Dengue—Indonesia—
Prevention. | Dengue—Treatment—Indonesia. | Public health—
Reasearch—Indonesia. | Medical cooperation—Indonesia |
Public-private sector cooperation—Indonesia.
Classification: LCC RA644.D4 F74 2024 |
DDC 614.5/885209598—dc23/eng/20240405
LC record available at https://lccn.loc.gov/2024008881

Printed in the United States of America

Cover design: Noah Arlow
Cover image: Shutterstock

To the Tahija Family and the World Mosquito
Program Yogyakarta Staff

CONTENTS

Preface   ix

Introduction: An Extraordinary Story   1

1 The Virus and the Mosquitoes   8

2 The Business Family: The Tahijas   26

3 The New Mosquitoes   45

4 The Partnership   61

5 More Stakeholders   79

6 The Community   94

7 The Community Volunteers: Women Lead the Way   122

8 The Results   144

9 Lessons for the Future   164

Acknowledgments   177
Notes   181
Index   201

PREFACE

A conversation with George Tahija, a University of Virginia Darden School of Business alum and supporter of many projects at the school, brought the Defeating Dengue project to the attention of coauthor R. Edward Freeman. He suggested that the project would make a great case study to use in class around issues of stakeholder engagement. Freeman then traveled to Indonesia in 2019 to write the case study about the project. The experience of meeting the family and team from the Tahija Foundation and University of Gadja Mada, going to a community engagement meeting, and seeing all the street art and excitement that surrounded the project convinced Freeman that there was much more to this project than could be captured in a short business school case study. He suggested to the family that they write a book about the project, as it was the most thorough stakeholder engagement project that he had ever seen.

Fast forward to 2020 and the onset of the COVID-19 pandemic. It was impossible to get anyone to travel to Indonesia to write the book, so the family asked Freeman if he would be the author. Freeman contacted Andrew Sell, a senior researcher at Darden's Institute for Business in Society, and together they embarked on writing this volume. The Tahija Foundation hired Rita Widiadana to interview the project participants, and Ibu Rita provided us with translated transcripts of the interviews with the participants and many key stakeholders. Freeman, Sell, and Joey Burton, executive director of the institute, interviewed the Tahija family on multiple occasions. Foundation CEO Trihadi Saptoadi and staff member Silvia Novi were invaluable in helping us bring this book project to completion.

Our greatest debt is to the family: Sjakon, Shelley, George, and Laurel Tahija for not only helping us but also having the courage to take on the project of defeating dengue fever and persevering over more than ten years to reach a successful and world-altering conclusion. And without the tireless work of Ibu Rita Widiadana, we would not have the insights of the many women and men who made the project possible.

We benefited greatly from the support of the Darden School and its Institute for Business in Society. Joey Burton was a hands-on member of our team. Megan Juelfs, Rebecca Little, Gaby Matheu, Jenny Mead, Ewshma Narula, and Salem Zelalem all contributed important research and feedback for the book. Our colleagues Megan Juelfs, Jenny Mead, Bidhan Parmar, Steve Momper, Maureen Wellen, and others offered friendly readings of earlier drafts. And our students who wrestled with the management issues in the early draft of the case study in Darden School dean Scott Beardsley's and Freeman's "Seminar on the Role of the CEO in the 21st Century" gave us several important ideas.

We were inspired by everyone at the World Mosquito Program Yogyakarta, from senior scientists to community volunteers. What they accomplished is unprecedented. And they built on the years of scientific research and community outreach of the World Mosquito Program Global team.

There is a long road ahead before we can end the scourge that is dengue fever. However, we can use the example of these courageous teams in Indonesia to push forward. And we can use the example of how this project created a network of stakeholders working together at national, regional, business, and local levels to tackle an important grand challenge.

DEFEATING DENGUE

INTRODUCTION

An Extraordinary Story

THE CHARACTERS AND THE STORIES

This book tells the remarkable tale of how a business family, the Tahijas of Indonesia, took on a dreaded disease, dengue fever, and resolved to defeat it. Throughout, multiple intertwined stories deliver a tale of struggle and triumph.

First, there is the story of the Tahija family and their commitment, as one of the leading business families in Indonesia, to wipe out the scourge of the dengue virus. Their values and philosophy, business and management acumen, and overall resilience are all central ingredients in their fight against dengue fever.

Second, there is an almost unbelievable story of a technology and scientific idea whereby the *Wolbachia* bacteria, which is common in many insect species and blocks the dengue virus, were injected into mosquitoes for release in affected areas. Again, the Tahija family's ability to shift their focus to the *Wolbachia*-infected mosquito through their philosophy of venture philanthropy is a key piece of the overall story.

Third, through its philanthropic arm, Yayasan Tahija (Tahija Foundation), the Tahija family assembled a multistakeholder partnership that consisted of the foundation, Gadja Madha University and medical school, the sultan of Yogyakarta, and many others whose buy-in was necessary if the project was to have any chance of success.[1] While multistakeholder partnerships are more common today, this one is remarkable for its diversity of interests, duration of more than ten years, and astonishing results.

Fourth, there is the story of leaders, citizens, and volunteers in the villages of Yogyakarta who joined together to make the project successful. The Tahija family galvanized an entire community to collaborate on an endeavor that took many years but, in the end, saved many lives. Their "hyper-local" approach—treating stakeholders as individual persons, not just fillers of functional roles—will be difficult to replicate. It requires that leaders step forward at all levels of the project, from top managers in the partnership to the volunteers in the villages.

As the stories from those involved were revealed to us, we realized that these narratives show how business families can contribute to the solutions to some of their society's most difficult problems. Groundbreaking science alone often cannot break through difficult obstacles to a meaningful societal impact without an ensemble cast of multidisciplinary teams, diligent multistakeholder engagement, and much more. And business families can lead the way.

The determined efforts of many stakeholders with a variety of skills, experience, and backgrounds—ten years and more in the making—eventually culminated in the triumphant near defeat of a deadly foe in the area. But the positive outcome from all their hard work was never certain, and seemingly insurmountable roadblocks frequently stood in their way. It took years of painstakingly difficult work, counterintuitive innovations, and intense relationship-building among stakeholder groups that were not always eager to work with one another to produce this incredible outcome. Rarely have the results of a scientific experiment been so uplifting for such a diverse group of people across all strata of society. And the potential societal impact could be transformative for many countries struggling with the society-wide wide impact of dengue fever—though it will likely take a diverse group of stakeholders in each country to capitalize on the innovative science behind developing *Wolbachia*-infected mosquitoes.

This scientific breakthrough was no accident. It was not based purely on luck. And it was not easy. It took many years of assiduous and sustained strategic planning, and it took the Tahija family's constant and unrelenting effort in nurturing and managing key partnerships and relationships across many stakeholders to transform an idea into a breakthrough—one that now has the potential to be transformational in the fight against dengue fever and other mosquito-borne diseases all over the world.

What follows is the historical background on key stakeholders; their motives for choosing to join the fight against dengue fever; their lived experiences while involved in a multiphase, ten-year project; and key lessons we took away from their sustained hard work and dedication. We weren't able to include all the individual stories from the thousands of people involved or do all their contributions justice in a single book (that wasn't thousands of pages long). But we hope that we can shed some much-warranted light on this incredible triumph against seemingly endless challenges in the fight to eliminate the scourge of dengue fever. We were amazed by their ingenuity, foresight, values, and tenacity in the face of numerous adversities. We think you will be amazed, too.

THE RESULTS

"Staggering"
"Epochal"
"Extraordinary"
"Huge promise"

These were just some of the reactions by scientists worldwide—a group not usually prone to using superlatives—when they heard about a field study's preliminary results that were officially released in August 2020.[2] These scientific findings were the result of a randomized controlled trial in Yogyakarta, Indonesia, that reduced dengue fever infection rates by an astounding 77 percent and hospitalization rates by 86 percent. The reactions from these scientists were understandable. And amid a terrible COVID-19 pandemic, the findings were a welcome respite from so much discouraging news.

The news of these scientific findings took only a day or two to spread swiftly across the globe, with much fanfare and jubilation by the press and infectious disease experts. But little did most people know how many years of blood, sweat, and tears it took to realize that result. Nearly a decade prior, three organizations had come together to form a long-term partnership, which became known as the World Mosquito Program Yogyakarta (WMPY): the Tahija Foundation, the University of Gadjah Mada, and the World Mosquito Program.[3] Their common goal was to see if an innovative new intervention method would be effective at preventing dengue fever. The Tahija family's foundation was the linchpin providing both funding and management expertise to the partnership. Without it, the partnership would have had no chance of success. Even so, during the project's ten-plus-year time frame, the partnership faced many hurdles and challenges, and no one knew whether or not there would be a positive outcome.

Thousands of people from across a broad swath of Indonesian society—scientists, Tahija Foundation members and staff, nonprofit organizations, government officials, public health administrators, and volunteers—joined in WMPY's efforts to conduct a series of increasingly complicated and broader field studies that culminated in some of the largest ever conducted.

To add to the challenges faced by the WMPY stakeholders, the complex, cutting-edge science employed in these studies also required convincing thousands of community members to participate in a rather strange experiment with a counterintuitive intervention method. These community members consented to releasing and helping monitor the birth of millions of mosquitoes in their own backyard—mosquitoes that were infected with bacteria from a laboratory.

For those who had been working on the project for many years, the results may have felt like the first warm rays of sunshine after interminable days of cloudy skies. They had faced many seemingly intractable obstacles and challenges over a decade—not the least of which was a global pandemic that threatened a twenty-seven-month field experiment and took the lives of many loved ones.

Many people from all walks of life and backgrounds had spent years dedicating their lives to discovering whether a promising new technology could effectively eliminate dengue fever when so many other solutions had failed. There was always a strong chance that it would not work, and not necessarily because the technology was not designed well. The bigger challenges were keeping a multisector international partnership strong for a decade or more while continuously working to convince several diverse stakeholders from across society (and countries) that a brand new, complicated, and counterintuitive approach to defeating dengue would really work.

And that is an important takeaway from the WMPY project. It is one thing to discover something new in a laboratory after several painstaking years of trial and error. But as many scientists know—and many of the scientists involved in this project attested to—it is highly unlikely that a scientific discovery will have meaningful impact if nobody outside the laboratory cares.

What can often be overlooked about any new technology or discovery is that for it to truly become a breakthrough for society, it must break through significant indifference, skepticism, and rejection. In other words, scientists need many nonscientists from various backgrounds to also step forward as supportive stakeholders in a new scientific endeavor for it to have a chance to achieve a seminal breakthrough for humanity. A great number of influential people and organizations need to see the possible benefits to themselves and others and to support a new scientific endeavor. And it is here that the Tahija family has played such a heroic role. They funded, managed, and shepherded the project for its entire duration. In short, they cared about eliminating dengue and making Indonesian society better.

Why would so many people spend so much time, treasure, and talent to try to eliminate dengue fever? That's the story we tell in the following chapters. In chapter 1, we outline the facts about dengue fever, the viruses that cause it, and the mosquitoes that carry it. In chapter 2, we get to know the Tahija family and see how their business values and philosophy were such a large a part of the project's success. In fact, they had begun the fight against dengue with an earlier technology that they felt had failed, but they persevered to learn important lessons that could be applied to the new attempt to eliminate dengue. Chapter 3 chronicles the plan to use mosquitoes infected with *Wolbachia* bacteria to attack the dengue problem. Chapter 4 is the story of the multistakeholder partnership put together by the Tahija Foundation and the challenges that the partnership faced. Chapter 5 examines many other stakeholders who got in on the act, including government agencies and the sultan of Yogyakarta, whose father was a friend of the Tahija family.

In chapter 6 we see how the WMPY team, consisting of the key players from the Tahija Foundation and the university, worked together to gain community support for the project. Leaders emerged at all levels of the project. Chapter 7 continues this story and focuses on the volunteers from the community who drove the execution of the project; here, many volunteer women took on leadership roles. Chapter 8 is a more detailed statement of the results, and chapter 9 suggests some lessons for businesses, members of the scientific community, and business families for tackling issues like dengue.

1

THE VIRUS AND THE MOSQUITOES

Esther looked on in anguish as her young daughter lay in bed. A severe headache, nausea, and muscle pain throughout her body kept the child bedridden during the day. Things only got worse at night. A fluctuating fever, sometimes rising to 40 degrees Celsius (104 degrees Fahrenheit), wracked her little body and made for a sleepless night for both. Esther knew that her daughter must have contracted what she had dreaded: dengue fever. These symptoms were too similar to her niece's symptoms from a week earlier. Her niece, whose face had turned a sickly and unnatural blue color before she was raced to the hospital, had been diagnosed with severe dengue fever—a life-threatening disease. Trembling, with her precious daughter's symptoms worsening, Esther rushed her daughter to the hospital, where her worst fears were confirmed: her daughter had severe dengue fever and would need to be closely monitored in the hospital for days. A dengue outbreak in 2016 in her neighborhood and nearby neighborhoods in Yogyakarta, Indonesia, had recently afflicted many others, and some had died from the virus.

Now Esther's daughter's and niece's lives hung in the balance, and dengue fever was not known for being forgiving to the children it infected. Globally, it is estimated that tens of thousands die from severe dengue each year—many of them children.[1] Unfortunately, the real-life tragedy that befell Esther's family in Indonesia is not uncommon in Indonesia. In fact, a 2014 study of urban children conducted in geographically dispersed areas in Indonesia found that more than 80 percent of children at least ten years old had been infected with dengue at least once—a staggeringly high percentage.[2] While Indonesia suffers one of the heaviest burdens from dengue fever, dengue's negative impact is widespread globally. Around the world, thousands of people die from the severe form of dengue fever every year. It can kill the young and the old, the sick and the healthy. According to the World Health Organization (WHO), dengue fever incidents have grown dramatically worldwide over the last few decades, with around four hundred million infections annually, and nearly four billion people are at risk across more than one hundred twenty-five countries.[3] In addition to the human burden of dengue, recent studies have estimated that dengue's global economic burden could be anywhere from USD$8.9 billion to USD$39.8 billion annually.[4] Given these sobering worldwide statistics, it should not be surprising that in recent years, WHO added dengue to its "ten threats to global health" that demand attention.[5]

For many countries dengue is the leading cause of illness.[6] Dengue infection cases have occurred on every continent except Antarctica, with outbreaks increasing around the world and spreading into new areas, including the United States (Florida, Texas)[7] and Europe (France, Italy, Spain).[8] Climate change, population growth, increased population densities via urbanization, and globalization combine to increase the incidence and geographic spread of this fatal virus. Current trends indicate that without dramatic human intervention dengue outbreaks will become far worse in the years ahead.[9]

MEET THE MAIN VILLAIN IN THIS STORY: THE DENGUE VIRUS

Dengue beats out malaria and other diseases as the "most common mosquito-borne viral disease in the world."[10] When people mention dengue fever, they are talking broadly about someone infected with one of four closely related RNA flavivirus serotypes known collectively as "dengue" and its most common symptom—fever—that some people exhibit while infected.[11] One of dengue's quirks is that if you are infected with one "serotype" (i.e., a distinct variation of the virus), not only are you not immune to the other serotypes of dengue virus during your lifetime, but your chances of experiencing severe symptoms (e.g., hemorrhaging, shock) when infected with another dengue serotype are actually higher. This means an individual can be infected with dengue up to four times in their lifetime, and, frighteningly, subsequent infections are more likely to be severe.

DENGUE'S LONG RAP SHEET

Symptomatic dengue results in two defined syndromes: dengue fever (DF) and dengue hemorrhagic fever (DHF) or dengue shock syndrome (DSS). While DF is a fairly simple illness, DHF is a severe and potentially life-threatening condition. DHF/DSS is characterized by a low blood platelet count, the result being dangerous bleeding. Severe, profound shock is known to occur in extreme cases and is associated with high mortality.

Unlike the COVID-19 virus, which recently caused a global pandemic, the dengue virus has a long history as a global affliction. In the tenth century, a Chinese medical encyclopedia mentioned a disease that had symptoms similar to dengue fever. It is suspected that dengue was the cause of outbreaks of illness in the Caribbean and Central America starting in the 1600s, introduced by new shipping routes to the Americas. Improved shipping technology and expanded trade routes in the eighteenth and nineteenth centuries increased dengue outbreaks in various regions, but epidemics were still fairly rare and typically occurred once a decade or longer.

Fast-forward to the years following World War II, when dengue's potency increased significantly in Southeast Asia due to rapid urbanization, improved transportation, and lack of effective mosquito controls. Researchers suspect that changing ecology in Southeast Asia contributed to the emergence of DHF/DSS. These trends continued at an even faster clip during the latter part of the twentieth century, with epidemics spreading so swiftly over large geographic expanses that dengue quickly became one of the twenty-first century's "most important infectious diseases affecting tropical urban areas."[12]

Scientists have come a long way in understanding dengue's dossier, as it has been investigated rigorously for decades. For example, it is now known that several environmental factors influence the likelihood and intensity of outbreaks in a region. Researchers have discovered that rainfall is highly correlated with the geographic distribution and timing of increased infection incidents; more rain typically means more dengue incidents. Climates that have a rainy season, such as most of Indonesia, are especially likely to experience outbreaks during times of high rainfall.

These environmental factors give dengue a diabolical boost, but there is a key enabling factor that dengue needs to infect people: it has accomplices.

MEET DENGUE'S ACCOMPLICES: AEDES AEGYPTI AND *AEDES ALBOPICTUS*

Two species of mosquitoes are known vectors (hosts) for the dengue virus. *Aedes aegypti* is the main host, although the virus can also be carried by *Aedes albopictus*. These *Aedes* genus mosquitoes can both live and reproduce in a broad range of climates, including tropical, subtropical, and even some temperate regions. They are also prolific and resourceful breeders, known to breed in a welter of everyday discarded items. Essentially anything that can hold a little bit of standing water will suffice—even something as small as a bottle cap is a viable breeding habitat. Perhaps even more disconcerting is the fact that their eggs can lie dry and unhatched for an entire year and still manage to hatch after coming in contact with water.[13]

To make matters worse, these species have dramatically expanded their ranges—to a large extent—because of globalization. These insects and their brood take advantage of globalized supply chains, hitching a ride in cargo or transportation, and can reach nearly anywhere in the world within just a few days. Global travel by infected humans can also quickly spread dengue if they have been bitten by a mosquito. These trends could help explain why, fifty years ago, only nine countries were reporting severe dengue outbreaks but more than one hundred twenty-five have reported that the disease is endemic.[14] In addition to human-enabled transportation expansion, there is also concern that warming in temperate regions from climate change may further increase the range of the primary carrier of dengue, *Ae. aegypti*, as it has not historically survived in areas with cold winter extremes.[15]

Dengue-infected *Aedes* mosquitoes transmit the virus when a female bites a person. (The females need blood to reproduce;

male mosquitoes do not bite animals or humans.) Typically biting during the day, *Ae. aegypti* often bites several people during its feeding period (i.e., an intermittent feeder), behavior that makes it an even more prolific dengue vector.[16] Interspecies transmission is essentially the only way dengue is spread; direct human-to-human transmission does not occur, though there is evidence of mother-to-infant transmission.[17]

THE HEALTH CONSEQUENCES OF DENGUE AND SEVERE DENGUE

Not all people who are infected with dengue show symptoms. An estimated 40–80 percent of dengue infections are asymptomatic.[18] But when symptoms do manifest, a common ailment is a fever accompanied by pain in the joints and bones that can get so severe that dengue fever has been given the moniker "breakbone fever."[19] Over many decades, scientists, researchers, and physicians have searched for effective treatments after someone is diagnosed with dengue and exhibits symptoms, but there remains no effective antiviral drug or globally approved vaccine. Instead, medical professionals concentrate on managing the symptoms of those infected. Treatment can take a variety of forms but primarily focuses on supporting patients' physical health by ensuring they stay hydrated with vital fluids ("fluid therapy"). Based on clinical observations, patients who experience symptoms after a five- to seven-day incubation period go through what are considered to be three typical sequential phases: febrile, critical, and convalescent.[20]

The febrile phase is characterized by an intense fever. In addition, many people suffer from eye, muscle, joint, and bone pain as well as a rash and hemorrhagic symptoms (e.g., bleeding gums) along with possibly many other unpleasant symptoms. This phase typically lasts from two days to a week.

According to the Mayo Clinic, some warning signs for and symptoms of severe dengue are severe abdominal pain; persistent vomiting; bleeding from the gums or nose; blood in the urine, stools, or vomit; bleeding under the skin, which may look like bruising; difficult or rapid breathing; cold or clammy skin (shock); fatigue; and irritability or restlessness.[21]

The critical phase is very short, typically lasting only one to two days. Most people recover after the febrile (i.e., fever) symptoms dissipate. However, a significant number of individuals suffer from severe dengue. Health professionals watch especially closely for warning signs related to shock, because if a patient goes into shock, mortality rates can increase by 10–40 percent without timely and adequate treatment.[22]

The incredibly short time frame of the critical phase—and its significantly increased mortality rate in the absence of timely medical treatment—illustrates the need for rapid access to high-quality medical diagnosis and support. Since symptoms of dengue could look similar to those of other illnesses, medical professionals prefer to rely on specific diagnostic laboratory tests to confirm the presence of the dengue virus in a patient's serum, plasma, blood, spinal fluid, or tissue.[23] And since a primary side effect of severe dengue is hemorrhaging, it is critical that a patient receive, as quickly as possible, enough oral or intravenous fluids—which may include platelet transfusions—to replace the vital fluids lost.[24] Time is of the essence when combating the devastating consequences of severe dengue.

The convalescent or recovery phase can last weeks. Hospital professionals have observed that patients take an average of almost seven weeks to completely recover the quality of life they had before contracting dengue fever, with gradual improvement over many weeks.[25] While many people do not suffer long-term persistent symptoms, some do have lingering side effects, including fever, headache, and nausea, with women more likely to experience long-term symptoms than men.[26]

Despite all that scientists and medical professionals have learned about this common virus, there remains no definitive cure, treatment, or vaccine to render it innocuous. Over the years an array of tactics have been employed by numerous stakeholders in an effort to eradicate dengue with varying degrees of success but no long-term victories.

WHO IS MOST AT RISK FOR DENGUE AND SEVERE DENGUE?

At the broadest level, living in a tropical or subtropical climate puts people most at risk for contracting any form of dengue. Some factors that increase the likelihood of dengue fever outbreaks include poor sanitation and waste management practices, which provide fertile ground for infected *Ae. aegypti* to multiply and spread dengue quickly.[27] It was once thought that dengue was confined to densely populated urban areas, but multiple studies have found that some rural areas can have higher rates of dengue infections.[28]

However, someone who has been previously infected with dengue (i.e., seropositive) is significantly more likely to experience severe dengue symptoms when infected again. It's estimated that about 95 percent of severe cases of dengue fever occur among those infected a second time.

One aspect of dengue that frightens many parents and caregivers is their children's high susceptibility to the severe and fatal forms. In many Southeast Asian countries, dengue is typically the leading cause of hospitalization and death for children.[29] Children also represent the majority of hospitalizations and account for the most recorded deaths from dengue.[30] The good news is that adequate and timely treatment can reduce the number of children dying from dengue to less than 1 percent (down from 20 percent if left untreated).

DENGUE IN INDONESIA

Indonesia is a diverse democratic nation with hundreds of ethnicities and more than seven hundred languages. It consists of over seventeen thousand islands of various sizes along the equator. While it is the world's fourth most populous country, with more than 250 million people, it is only the sixteenth largest in terms of geographic area—and a considerable amount of that is water or uninhabited islands. In addition, agricultural land (31 percent) and the world's largest number of active volcanoes means there is not an overabundance of habitable land. In fact, some of the most densely populated areas in the world are on the island of Java, whose population is estimated at over 130 million (well over half Indonesia's total population, but only about 7 percent of its land area). And over 50 percent of its population lives in an urban environment, with urbanization increasing every year (over 2 percent) as rural residents decide to move to cities.[31] Indonesia is also the largest majority Muslim country in the world.

After gaining its independence from colonial Dutch rule shortly after World War II, Indonesia had two presidents, Sukarno until 1965 and Suharto from 1965 to 1998. In 1998, the country moved to a more democratic and decentralized system of government. Many government functions were moved to regional governments.

Near the equator and surrounded by warm ocean water, Indonesia has a tropical monsoonal climate. This type of climate often produces high humidity and rainfall, which are positively correlated with dengue cases. While becoming infected with dengue is possible throughout the year in most of Indonesia, dengue cases increase during the rainy season, which can vary by year and location but is typically between September and February, lasting around six months.[32] Combine all these factors, and it is not hard to understand why mosquitoes and the dengue virus thrive in Indonesia.

Even though dengue fever has been around for a long time, the first official reports of dengue outbreaks in Indonesia were in 1968, in Jakarta and the East Java region. It afflicted fifty-eight patients with acute fever and hemorrhaging, with a shockingly high 80 percent fatality rate (this rate is much, much lower now, fortunately). Since then, dengue infections have become highly prevalent and widespread throughout most regions of Indonesia.[33]

The recent COVID-19 pandemic has not helped matters related to dengue fever in Indonesia and other Southeast Asian countries. Government lockdowns meant to reduce COVID-19 transmissions may have played a role in notable increases in dengue infections in the region. During the summer of 2020, health officials in several Southeast Asian countries, including Indonesia, saw dramatic increases in dengue fever cases. Unfortunately, it appears that one unintended consequence of trying to stop COVID-19 from spreading inadvertently aided dengue, or as one physician more colorfully put it, "Unfortunately dengue met the best marriage partner—lockdown."[34]

Commenting for a news article as to why doctors may be seeing an influx of dengue fever cases during the pandemic, Dr. Duane Gubler, founding director of the Emerging Infectious

Diseases Signature Research Programme at Duke-NUS Medical School in Singapore, mentioned that "people who are stuck at home all the time probably have greater contact with mosquitoes that are infected with dengue." Experts speculated that people forced to stay home were being exposed for longer durations to infected mosquitoes in their neighborhoods. Also, lockdown-induced delays left construction sites unfinished, with plenty of unattended places for standing water to pool.

The chances of dying from dengue fever have generally declined in Indonesia as health professionals have learned how to treat it since that first well-documented instance in 1968. Indonesia's dengue fever fatality rate is approximately 1 percent, but some nonurban areas have reported rates as high as 3–5 percent.[35] This higher fatality rate in nonurban areas suggests that people in these areas bear a greater burden due to lack of adequate medical attention during dengue's critical phase.

Throughout Indonesia, dengue continues be a significant societal burden and daily concern. The disease's overall impact has only gotten worse. Severe cases have been trending upward over the last fifty years; for example, in 1968, there were only 0.5 cases per 100,000 people compared with 2016, which had approximately 78 cases per 100,000 people.[36] And Indonesia suffers one of the highest cost burdens of any country in terms of hospitalizations and ambulatory care due to dengue infections.[37]

VARIOUS STRATEGIES TO ELIMINATE DENGUE

Over the decades, several dengue prevention and eradication strategies were tried, with varying degrees of success; none had achieved sustained effectiveness over the long term. Active disease surveillance in the health care system can help alert health authorities to emerging dengue outbreaks. However, this strategy requires laboratory-based resources to positively identify dengue infections—since its symptoms (e.g., high fever) are similar to those of other common infectious diseases—as well as rapid data-sharing coordination with public health authorities to alert them to outbreaks so they can take remedial action.

Given the considerable resources, infrastructure, and systems needed to operate and sustain an active dengue surveillance system, it is difficult for developing countries like Indonesia to initiate and maintain effective systems. Also, while a surveillance system may help reduce the severity of dengue fever outbreaks, it does not address the root cause of dengue: dengue-infected mosquitoes. Three other dengue prevention and eradication strategies have been used, sometimes in tandem with an active dengue surveillance system: vaccines, insecticides, and modification of human behavior.

Vaccines

It has been very difficult for scientists to develop an effective dengue virus vaccine. In contrast to the incredibly quick turnaround time for developing effective vaccines against the SARS-CoV-2 coronavirus (the virus responsible for the COVID-19 pandemic)—which took less than a year to develop and receive governmental approval—scientists have been working on a vaccine for dengue for decades, with little success. The challenges they face are based on several factors peculiar to dengue. Dengue has four distinct serotypes, and being infected with one serotype does not make you immune to the other three in the long term, though there does seem to be extremely short-term cross-serotype protection for a few months after infection.[38] And, importantly, becoming infected with a serotype different from the first increases the odds that you will experience severe symptoms, a phenomenon known as "antibody-dependent enhancement of infection."[39] In other words, the antibodies from the first infection actually help the virus replicate when you are infected with a different serotype. This increases the difficulty for vaccine developers because they need to adequately protect those who are inoculated from all four dengue serotypes simultaneously.

Given these challenges, it is not surprising that to date, only one vaccine has been approved in some countries. In addition, because of safety concerns, there are often many restrictions on who is approved to receive it. In 2015, Sanofi Pasteur, Inc., was approved to license the Dengvaxia® vaccine first in Mexico; since then, other countries have followed suit.[40] The vaccine consists of weakened yellow fever virus that contains certain genes of each of the four dengue virus serotypes.[41] The developers tried to address all four of dengue's serotypes at once with this approach. However, Dengvaxia® has been found to increase the risk of experiencing severe dengue symptoms if the person had never been infected with dengue prior to being vaccinated. (This is known in the medical field as being "seronegative" for dengue.) For those never before infected with dengue, the vaccine seems to act as if it were infecting them for the first time (even though the vaccine doesn't actually infect them with dengue)—which has the unfortunate side effect of increasing the risk of severe dengue if the person is infected after being vaccinated. Overall, the limitations of this vaccine have caused confusion, controversy, and severely limited its effectiveness in preventing dengue fever infections globally. Other vaccines are in developmental stages, but none is commercially available.

Insecticides

One common strategy governments use against dengue is to initiate localized insecticide spraying ("fogging") to kill mosquitoes hosting the virus. While this prevention strategy can be expensive and prompt community pushback due to environmental concerns, the practice is prevalent because its visibility gives community members a greater sense of security and government actionability (the government is doing something about dengue). Policies and practices have favored unilateral strategies with a single eradication method, relying solely on insecticide application.[42] Once dengue has been controlled in certain areas, governments frequently reduce their efforts and funding for fogging there. Unfortunately, since the mosquitoes are never fully eradicated in surrounding areas, the mosquito population rebounds over time and dengue outbreaks return to the treated area.[43]

This dengue prevention approach also can lead to a false sense of security, as the insecticide cannot reach all places where mosquitoes reside (e.g., inside peoples' homes). And where it does reach, it kills only the adult mosquitoes, allowing the eggs to hatch and spread rapidly. Overall, many consider fogging to be an ineffective dengue eradication technique.[44]

A top-down dengue eradication initiative, such as government fogging, allows for greater control over the entire process and the resources allocated (e.g., funding, personnel) to fund a finite project. However, it puts all the responsibility on the government to solve the dengue problem, and mosquito populations have proven to be far too resilient. Given a lack of sustainable success with fogging, governments and their partners have been implementing more community-based approaches that aim to eradicate dengue by modifying collective human behavior.

Modification of Human Behavior

Modifying human behavior can take many forms, including having people regularly remove standing water (prime mosquito egg-laying habitat) in their homes and on their property, restricting travel, using personal protection (e.g., netting, insect repellent), and more closely monitoring and tracking dengue infections through surveillance coordinated with medical professionals.

Many governments have implemented educational and training programs with the goal of improving community awareness of dengue fever and what actions people can take to prevent it or ameliorate its effects. While government programs to improve community participation in dengue prevention are well intentioned and likely necessary for any comprehensive solution, they can be difficult and expensive to administer. Also, often it has been difficult to get enough community members to participate in sustainable dengue prevention best practices.

Listening to, and attempting to address, the common concerns community members have about dengue prevention practices can help health officials develop more effective social and behavioral change campaigns. These public health campaigns have the potential to boost community participation and a sense of ownership to help prevent future dengue fever outbreaks. However, experts also started to appreciate that a top-down-only approach—be it government-led chemical spraying or educational programs—was not going to be enough to eliminate dengue. Sustained community participation was always too low to have a significant and lasting impact on stopping dengue infections. To have a fighting chance of eliminating the threat of dengue, bottom-up, community-based engagement was needed.[45] It took several decades of failed top-down interventions for experts to start to build a consensus that strong bottom-up programs were necessary for a sustainable approach to eliminating dengue.

Over time more collaborative and integrative strategies have emerged, with governments more likely to partner with other organizations to coordinate top-down along with bottom-up strategies in the fight against dengue. An example of a top-down program is a government agency systematically spraying insecticides in habitat that is known to harbor dengue-infected mosquitoes. A bottom-up initiative would be a coordinated community-based program whereby members try to control mosquito populations through their own actions, such as eliminating standing water on their property and/or helping to monitor dengue infections so they can be contained before a large outbreak occurs.

Although the Indonesian government has initiated national health education programs, it has not developed any national immunization programs to combat dengue. A lack of such programs may be because they would be expensive to administer. It also may be due to the fact that the only dengue vaccine widely available, Dengvaxia, has the aforementioned accompanying risks and concerns.

Indonesian governmental intervention trends largely mirrored global activities starting in 1968, when dengue was first documented in the country. The national government, spearheaded by the Ministry of Health, made studying, monitoring, and striving to prevent and control dengue a priority. Control of the virus primarily started with vertical, top-down programs such as chemical spraying in dengue hotspots from the late 1960s through the 1980s. Concurrently, physicians were being trained to better diagnose and manage DHF starting in the 1970s. These programs had limited success in preventing dengue. Beginning in the 1990s, the government has focused more on developing partnerships with stakeholders across sectors and on more bottom-up, community-based programs.[46]

After decades of lessons learned from fighting dengue, in the early twenty-first century, consensus was building among a wide group of experts that integrated multistrategy, intersectoral campaigns were needed to effectively fight dengue—and that community participation was essential for sustainable prevention.[47] In 2012, WHO developed its integrated vector management (IVM) handbook to provide guidance for stakeholders interested in controlling mosquito populations with the aim of "making vector control more efficient, cost effective, ecologically sound and sustainable."[48] It was better understood that a complex set of socioecological factors caused dengue outbreaks and that a single top-down government solution had no chance of eradicating dengue in the long term. Effective dengue eradication strategies would need to include multiple stakeholders, multiple sectors, and multiple eradication methods to have any chance at lasting success. Those who have tried these integrative initiatives to eliminate dengue understand that is extremely difficult to coordinate an effective multipronged top-down and bottom-up campaign to sustainably defeat dengue. The Tahija Foundation discovered all these challenges first hand when it supported its first ambitious project to eliminate dengue in Yogyakarta, Indonesia.

Esther's daughter and niece rebounded from their bout with dengue fever, but many other Indonesian children have not. Even when loved ones recover, it can be an excruciatingly painful experience for those afflicted and those who have to watch them suffer. So many families in Indonesia had loved ones and neighbors who suffered from dengue fever; it was like an ever-present, dark, and foreboding storm cloud over the country.

The Tahija Foundation and its leadership knew it would be difficult to eliminate dengue fever in Indonesia—after all, the national government had been trying for decades—but they also thought it was a worthwhile endeavor. They wanted families like Esther's, and many other Indonesian families (including their own), to avoid having to suffer from dengue. They were interested in investing in new ideas to defeat dengue in Indonesia.

2

THE BUSINESS FAMILY
The Tahijas

Imagine you live in Sumatra's Riau Province. Your house is made of palm leaves. Your children have little hope of finishing high school. You sometimes do not have enough food and you know many people who are worse off. You lie in bed at night worrying whether anything will change. You see few possibilities. Across the river is an American oil camp where people live well beyond your imagination. You know they are taking extraordinary wealth out of the land—Indonesian land, your land. You accept their success and comfort as somehow part of the natural order. They accomplish things that you could never dream of doing. But you do not want to be excluded and you expect to be treated fairly. You do not care what taxes the company pays to the central or regional government. You care about what the company does for you and your family.

—Julius Tahija, *Horizon Beyond*

THE TAHIJAS & YAYASAN TAHIJA

Julius Tahija was a remarkable man. He was a decorated war hero, a patriot and founder of the country while serving as a politician (post–World War II), as well as an accomplished business executive.[1] Julius set a high standard for his family to follow. He had a clear vision about the role of business in society, and in Indonesian society in particular: "A company can remain viable only if it serves social ends and can serve social ends only if it remains economically viable. Profits must be made and dividends must be paid. But social responsibility is a core part of business. The private sector can no longer think only in terms of profits and dividends."[2] And Tahija lived his life following this ethic of service and humility, especially with those who were less fortunate than he and his family. His wife, Jean, writes, "I have seen Julius go out of his way to help people who were more or less strangers to him, but who he felt deserved a chance in life. He has always been aware that his life, in some ways, has been privileged, and that he has a duty to help those less fortunate."[3]

Throughout his career as a Caltex oil executive and an entrepreneur building Tahija family businesses in such diverse industries as shipping, mining, manufacturing, insurance, banking, plantations, and commodities trading, Julius saw community development as a crucial part of the social obligations of any business. Community development meant being involved and engaged in the local communities where the businesses operated. In addition to supporting local businesses in job creation, companies needed to invest "in worker skills, protection of the environment, and minimizing inequities in distribution of income."

Tahija also had strong views about the role of ethics and values in business. As managing director of Caltex Indonesia, he worked hard to inculcate the idea that ethics and business must work in harmony. While Tahija recognized that Indonesian culture also played a big part in business philosophy, he says, "unethical practices waste resources, discourage investment, cut productivity and foster local businesses whose success is only temporary—exactly what a developing country can least afford."[4]

His son, George, who followed Julius into a business career, describes his father's business philosophy and values as follows: "The values formally emerged in an official value statement decades after my father conducted honest and fair business practices. His own journey of deciding what "honest and fair" meant was a product of his childhood and adult professional experiences across and including, Indonesian, Dutch, Chinese, American and Australian cultures."[5]

Speaking of an early occasion when officials tried to bribe him, his wife Jean writes, "This was a moment of truth for Julius, one that would determine the way he conducted business for the rest of his life. He knew that corruption was widespread and that paying what amounted to a bribe would undoubtedly smooth over some of the problems Caltex was experiencing. But he also knew that once he crossed that line there would be no turning back, that he would be caught in a web of corruption from which he could never extricate himself."[6]

George explains further. "My father was very adamant that a handshake agreement meant a commitment beyond any legal document. In the post–World War II days, he was struck by traders in Jakarta's Chinatown, who would carry pieces of paper in their pockets to write IOU's amongst themselves as transaction payment guarantees. The handwritten note and handshake was a sufficient bond. Such was the power of trust within the community that allowed business to be done quickly and practically, provided one had the reputation for integrity."[7]

Jean Tahija (née Walters) was born in 1916 in a suburb outside Melbourne, Australia. Her working-class parents were determined that she would have access to higher education, which was rare for any woman at that time. To help pay for Jean's college education, her mother bought a knitting machine and started selling knitted merchandise from her home. Aware of the financial burden that her education was having on her family, Jean switched to a degree in dental science soon after entering college, since it would shorten her education by one year. After five years of study, Jean graduated from the University of Melbourne in 1941 with a degree in dental science—the only woman in her cohort of twenty-four. Soon after graduating, she landed a job at the Melbourne Dental Hospital.[8]

When Jean started working, World War II was dramatically impacting people's lives throughout Australia. She and her family were no exception. Jean's brothers were off at war, and Jean was often working on soldiers' teeth, as many were stationed in Melbourne between deployments. Many of these soldiers asked her to go on dates while she practiced her dentistry, but Jean was not interested. She wanted to focus only on her career until later, in 1942, when she met a man named Julius Tahija, then a sergeant in the Royal Netherlands East Indies Army, who was stationed in Melbourne.[9] Julius had recently arrived in Australia after his unit had transported Japanese civilian internees to Australia from the island of Java.[10]

During the remainder of the war, Jean and Julius rarely were able to see each other, as Julius was frequently deployed on dangerous military assignments for many weeks at a time. But this lack of time together only seemed to strengthen their resolve to be together after the war ended—whenever that would be. Finally, after several long and stressful years, World War II ended in 1945. Julius continued his service in the Dutch East Indies Army until 1946 after being elected to the State of East Indonesia parliament, a new state established by the Netherlands after the war. In November 1946, Jean and Julius were married in Melbourne. Julius had to leave for Jakarta the day after the wedding to fulfill his governmental duties, while Jean had to wait five more months before receiving permission from the Australian and Dutch governments to be able to join her husband in East Indonesia.[11]

In Indonesia, Jean resumed her dentistry practice in Jakarta until their first child, Sjakon, was born in 1952.[12] By that time, Julius had transitioned out of government and military service and into his true passion: business. In 1951, he had taken a position at Caltex Pacific Indonesia, an American oil company, and rose up the ranks to become its CEO in 1966.[13] According to the family, Jean was an important influence in his success in business. "She was consistently a good judge of character, brought an international perspective, had a much-appreciated sense of humor, and maintained a balanced perspective on life."[14]

As Jean and Julius raised a family in Indonesia, they passed their views on business, social responsibilities, and values along to their two sons, Sjakon and George. All the Tahija family members have been adamant that business has an important role to play in Indonesia's development, and that business leaders need to take an active role in crafting solutions to Indonesia's many problems. Julius advocated this view for many years, which sometimes put him at odds with the Indonesian government. However, after the failed Communist coup in 1965, Indonesia was opened up to foreign investment, and businesses—especially family businesses—began to assume a larger role in the development of the national economy.

Business families play an important role in many Asian economies. In Indonesia, 95 percent of all enterprises are run by families, and some of the largest are the results of families that have built businesses in multiple industries and over multiple generations.

Over the years the Tahija family and its businesses grew and matured. George was in charge of the businesses that had investments in palm oil, energy, food, banking, and other sectors. Sjakon was a successful ophthalmologist with a special interest in health issues, and he was also involved in family business decisions. Shelley Tahija, Sjakon's wife, was a physician by training and occupation, specializing in pathology. Laurel Tahija, George's wife, with a master's degree from Johns Hopkins University School of International Studies, had a successful career in international banking. In 1995, she pursued her passion in improving local education by starting an innovative K–12 primary school in Jakarta and serving as its founder and treasurer.

All these Tahija family members (figure 2.1) strongly believed in giving back to their local communities. As they became more prominent in those communities, family members frequently

FIGURE 2.1 Portraits of the Tahija business family (L-R): Sjakon, Shelly, Laurel, and George.

received donation requests of all kinds, including for paying medical bills for individuals in need, building houses of worship, providing jobs for individuals or their family members, supporting natural disaster recovery efforts, and much more. However, the family had no formal policies, procedures, or staff dedicated to handling and vetting these requests for financial support.

These numerous and varied requests became difficult to manage, and it was challenging to determine which requests were genuine versus opportunistic. There were no strategies for charitable giving, and each family member had their own pet projects, rarely coordinating their activities to improve Indonesia through charitable funding. Overall, these charitable efforts lacked focus, coordination, and accountability. Sjakon and George pushed to formalize the family's various charitable activities.

In 1990, Jean and Julius established Yayasan Tahija (Tahija Foundation), based in Jakarta, to serve as a formal vehicle for the family's philanthropic initiatives.[15] Sjakon and George were involved in leading the nonprofit organization at its start and continued the family legacy after their parents' passing. The Tahija Foundation was built on the Tahijas' view of the necessity for business—especially business families—to play a part in the development of Indonesia. And the ethic of service to those less fortunate and humility continue to serve as the basic philosophy for the family and its foundation.

The entire family worked together in the foundation, whose stated purpose was "To bring about a better Indonesia through partnership for sustainable initiatives in education, culture, health, environmental conservation and social services."[16] The Tahija Foundation was not the only vehicle for giving back to the community. The family had established other projects to support philanthropy in education, environmental conservation, health, social services, and other areas.

The family believed that like the Tahija businesses, the foundation should exemplify their values. As foundation manager Victorius Munasdi, WMPY stakeholder liaison, put it, "The Tahija family's values of compassion, tolerance, generous but humble were contagious. Most of us felt appreciated. They required us to work harder but they also recognized our accomplishments. . . . Therefore, all the staff must amplify all the values of the collaboration—trust, honesty and integrity—because they are the ones who will directly interact with the people, the government officials and other stake holders."[17] These values were not only for the foundation but were critical in the Tahija family businesses. George said, "The soul of our organization is our culture and underpinning values. We would never tolerate anyone or anything that would compromise either."[18]

This culture was built on values that went far beyond just words. The family created a system of "values champions," whose job it was to facilitate discussions and solutions when the values were challenged. Two people, including George Tahija, were designated as values guardians, who would receive reports from the values champions "consisting of what activities were observed that enhanced or detracted from our values. The VC and VG system is run together with a whistleblower system which is anonymous."[19]

And in keeping with the long-standing principles articulated by Julius Tahija, the foundation refused to participate in bribery or other corruption activities. Finance executive Sonny Susanto said, "We're very worried about [corruption] and we cannot close our eyes that such practice exists. But we try hard not to get involved in any bribery. Our values are very strict, we don't do bribery. It's sometimes become an obstacle for us, like waiting for a permit which may take a long time to be issued, since we don't bribe—better to wait a long time than having to do it. Of course, it means extra cost, extra energy, and extra time but that's okay, it's the risk to uphold our values."[20]

Shelly Tahija put it this way: "Essential family values are the foundation for the operations of all institutions at Tahija Enterprise. These values become guidelines for everyone who works within the scope of Tahija Enterprise in carrying out their work and perhaps also in their personal lives. We always strive for these values both through various workshops and in daily activities."[21]

George Tahija viewed the Tahija Foundation as helping the family fulfill its mission to help build Indonesia: "I see the foundation and business serving our mission of elevating Indonesia in different and unique ways. Our 'reach' is greater having the Tahija Foundation. In a developing country where the government has limited means, nonprofits can play an important partnership role in achieving social good. The Tahija Foundation could not operate without funding and management experience from our for-profit activities. It's a symbiotic relationship that strengthens the presence, legacy, and reputation of the family in Indonesia."[22]

The 2004 Boxing Day tsunami provided a seminal moment in the family's philanthropic strategy. The Tahija Foundation adopted an Indonesian village, where it set up medical and educational facilities and built schools and much-needed clinics. It worked with experts at a local university to design and build earthquake-proof structures and train teachers. Using local resources and expertise helped the Tahija Foundation both address the tsunami-ravaged area and foster a sense of community involvement and ownership. Also during this time, the Tahija family and its foundation became more interested in addressing the persistent public health issues caused by dengue fever.

For the Tahijas, the pain of dengue fever hit close to home. Like Esther, mentioned in chapter 2, Sjakon's and Shelley's daughter had suffered the debilitating effects of dengue. Through the Tahija Foundation, they could try to take action so other Indonesian families would not have to experience the same pain. George and Laurel were also intrigued by the idea of tackling dengue fever. Their foundation had funded many social impact projects over the years, but family members wanted to refocus their efforts on high-impact initiatives that had the potential for a transformational outcome for Indonesian society. Successfully eradicating dengue fever would fit that bill. Dengue impacted all levels of society in Indonesia and had been a significant societal burden for decades with no signs of a solution in the absence of a new kind of intervention. The foundation could lead the way in this important fight against a societal-level problem. If the sons' families could make progress on inhibiting dengue fever, it would be a fitting legacy for their generation and a tribute to honor their parents, Julius and Jean Tahija.

After some discussion, consensus was reached that taking on dengue fever was the way forward. In the early 2000s, the family spoke with international experts to determine which promising interventions were available. Eventually a plan was developed for an ambitious field study that would employ new ways to eliminate dengue in local communities. It began in earnest in 2004. The Tahija Foundation, as a local, nongovernmental organizational (NGO), would be primarily responsible for implementing a new water treatment intervention in designated local communities. The foundation and other involved stakeholders called this endeavor the Sumilarv project.[23] The main equation for the desired outcome of this project was straightforward: no mosquitoes = no dengue fever.

Considerable time, talent, and funding were leveraged to determine whether this water treatment technique could put a big dent in the mosquito population, which all involved predicted would significantly reduce dengue infections. During the multiyear study, the Tahija Foundation hired and trained hundreds of local staff to implement such a large-scale study in the city of Yogyakarta, Indonesia.

Would this innovative method to fight dengue in Indonesia work as predicted? Decades of ineffective interventions that were primarily top-down government programs never eliminated dengue fever for an extended period in any location.

Consensus was growing among experts that programs that successfully promoted significant and sustained community participation (bottom-up design) were the only viable solution for eliminating dengue in an area. Top-down solutions, if they had a significant effect, had only temporary success at tamping down dengue infections. However, there was recognition that bottom-up programs would be complicated and resource intensive, involving many stakeholders and strong relationships among them, as "continuous effort by the community" would be needed if they were to have a real chance to eliminate dengue in a sizable area. With that in mind, a coalition of researchers, government officials, and NGOs (like the Tahija Foundation) conducted research in Yogyakarta, Indonesia, to examine the effectiveness of social interventions to improve community participation in dengue prevention practices and a new water treatment intervention aimed at reducing mosquito larvae numbers.[24] Some of the stakeholders discovered that some interventions worked as hoped, while others most certainly did not.

The Indonesian government agencies, along with domestic and international researchers, had been trying to eradicate dengue for decades. Would the Tahija Foundation and this new coalition of stakeholders finally find a durable solution against dengue in Indonesia? No. Not this time. But it was far from a complete failure. There were significant secondary benefits to the community, important lessons were learned along the way, and a foundation was built for future success.

A FAILURE OFTEN TEACHES THE BEST LESSONS

Sometimes you learn the most valuable lessons even when (or even because) you fail to accomplish your goals. The Tahija Foundation discovered this firsthand when it spearheaded the state-of-the-art water treatment intervention to control mosquito populations in Yogyakarta in an effort to eliminate dengue fever. The foundation was a prominent NGO stakeholder in multiyear field studies (2004–2010) which included several cross-sector partners (e.g., the CDC Foundation) and experts, who devised a study to investigate the effectiveness of social and water treatment interventions in eliminating dengue fever infections. The specific neighborhood-level intervention the Tahija Foundation spearheaded used complex data modeling that measured optimal water temperatures prior to the administration of a chemical, pyriproxyfen, that would reduce mosquito larvae populations—which should then, in theory, reduce dengue fever infections.

The Tahija Foundation was well known and trusted by the local community. It took responsibility for the water treatment intervention aspect of the study; it was a massive undertaking. It hired two hundred staff, who worked with local community members and research staff for a year in two of the targeted neighborhoods to utilize their expertise in treating the water at the optimal time to reduce mosquito larvae populations. Information on how to use the water treatment chemicals was also provided to community health center officials, local village leaders, and community members via a variety of local media outlets, such as radio and newspapers. And these studies were not small. The larger of the two field studies involved more than one hundred thousand households and five hundred thousand people in the Yogyakarta area.

The result of all this work from the Tahija Foundation and its partners was fewer larvae. But, counterintuitively, ultimately more mosquitoes and more dengue fever cases were found in the chemical intervention areas[25]—certainly a disappointing outcome for all those involved.

However, that is not the whole story. Even though the cutting-edge scientific chemical intervention did not significantly reduce dengue infections, rich and important findings emerged from the study. The community participation and stakeholder management aspect of the larger study were successes. An international research team—including scientists from the World Health Organization, University of Gadjah Mada (Indonesia), and University of Gothenburg (Sweden)—focused on other neighborhoods that would receive other "community-centered dengue eco-system management" interventions.[26]

This bottom-up model for tackling dengue fever, which involved significant community participation and sustained cross-sector partnerships, would also be considered a "horizontal" approach to eliminating dengue fever. In contrast to a vertical approach, whereby a single entity (e.g., the government) has sole responsibility to eliminate dengue fever, a horizontal approach describes an arrangement whereby multiple strategic partners, with relatively similar levels of authority, share responsibility on project outcomes and develop solutions collaboratively. It was also bottom-up in that many community members were actively involved in some aspects of the design of the intervention protocols and were needed as collaborators during the experiment. In fact, they were key stakeholders in the entire study. If the community did not participate, there was no chance that the study could achieve its goal of reducing dengue infections.

The larger study in which the Tahija Foundation's water intervention was embedded also included four neighborhoods that never received chemical. These additional neighborhoods were introduced to social interventions whose aim was to improve community engagement in dengue fever preventive practices. Some of the multistakeholder community engagement interventions included the following.[27]

- Identifying and working with local community leaders.
- Hosting community events, community-led forums, and neighborhood assemblies.
- Reaching out to involve a diverse set of groups in the neighborhoods, including women's associations and schools.
- Partnering with a multisector set of stakeholders with complementary domain expertise and local knowledge, including health institutions, public utilities, local political officials, and NGOs.
- Developing tools that supported communication and awareness campaigns in the neighborhood.

Another research objective was to systematically investigate whether a more bottom-up, community-empowering mosquito control strategy would effectively and sustainably reduce dengue infections in six Yogya neighborhoods. The research team developed strategies to increase involvement by empowering local community members to lead and organize efforts to eliminate dengue through solutions that worked best in their specific communities. Some key results from the interventions included these:

- Improved community knowledge and attitudes about engaging in dengue prevention practices that coincided with increased community participation in dengue prevention practices.
- Improved stakeholder partnerships and relationships that suggested a more sustainable dengue prevention ecosystem.
- Introduced household and community behavior that not only tackled mosquito control practices but also addressed environmental and health issues (e.g., waste management) in the community.

What these results brought home to those involved in the study was just how important it was to bring the neighborhood households together and instill in them a sense of community ownership and empowerment in the process—even if the particular scientific intervention they tested did not work the first time. The researchers who rigorously studied the impact of these community participation activities concluded that these bottom-up, community-based approaches—while more effortful at the beginning for the stakeholder groups—had better potential for long-term sustainability as opposed to a top-down approach.

The Tahija Foundation staff and other research study members helped organize a community celebration shortly after the overall study concluded to recognize all the positive progress and goodwill engendered with the communities. During the event, several community members commented on how their neighborhood felt safer and cleaner as an outcome of the study. Others mentioned how impressive an undertaking it had been, how engaged the community was, and how empowering it felt for them. As one community leader expressed it, "The project taught us that we had to take care of ourselves."[28]

Former Tahija Foundation chief executive officer Anastasius Wahyuhadi attended the community celebration to officially recognize the project's hundreds of volunteers and contract workers with certificates of appreciation. He extended an apology that the project was ending due to the disappointing scientific results.[29] At first he felt sad and uneasy at having to deliver this discouraging news; however, his spirits lifted as attendees shared their stories about what the project had meant to them and thanked the Tahija Foundation for providing them with the opportunity to participate in such an important project. Former employees had already established an association whose members received support on how to start up home-based economic activities, open retail shops, and become a consultant.

One woman shared her story with the assembled crowd about how, as a poor and uneducated housewife, she never would have dreamed of entering a building on the University of Gadjah Mada's campus (where training sessions occurred) or a rich person's home (to try to recruit them as study participants). She felt her life was totally changed—for the better—after her training and learning about the Tahija family's core values as a Sumilarv project volunteer. The training she received and her project-based experiences equipped her with managerial and communication skills to start operating a village-scale, wedding-organizing business. "Don't worry about us," she told Wahyuhadi. "We'll be fine."

The community event ended with music, dance, and theater performances by the former Sumilarv project employees. Community empowerment appeared to be one unexpected positive side effect of this so-called failed Sumilarv experiment.

Titayanto Pieter, the former general manager of the Sumilarv project in Yogyakarta, summarized additional positive effects.

> There were so many inspiring stories from our former workers that really humbled me. We did not realize that the project had transformed people's lives for the better, which is in line with the Tahija Family's values. . . . All staff was required to have bank accounts at Bank Niaga. On average, they were paid around Rp 800,000 (equivalent to US$800 per month) at the minimum, which was big enough for Yogyakarta people at that time. So, their salaries will be disbursed directly to their accounts. Having bank accounts was something strange for them. They had never had any bank accounts before. The majority of our front-line workers were ordinary housewives who had little knowledge about the banking system. This financial arrangement has changed social and economic dynamic of the women and their families. They practiced financial management as well as personal and family management. It was something they have never done before since they lived day by day, the money they earned gone on the same day. Now they had saving accounts.[30]

Through this study the researchers and the Tahija Foundation gained valuable knowledge of how critical community engagement, relationship building, and neighborhood buy-in is for implementing such a monumentally challenging scientific experiment. And they knew that the relationships forged in the various multisector stakeholder groups were valuable and that perhaps the formation of these strong relationships would be critical for a future attempt to eliminate dengue fever. And what is often forgotten about scientific inquiry is that science and experimentation is about trial and error. If at first you don't succeed, learn from your actions, adjust accordingly, and try again.

From this expensive and years-long undertaking, the study participants learned what worked: community involvement, multisector partnerships, and trust building. And just as importantly, they learned what didn't work: attempting to eliminate dengue by striving to eradicate mosquitoes with water treatment or water removal techniques. The Tahijas decided to present these negative results, and Sjakon did so before the American Society of Tropical Medicine and Hygiene. Sjakon Tahija summarized an important lesson: "With our presentation, we put the last nail in the coffin of mosquito eradication [as a strategy for eliminating mosquito borne illness]. . . . We proved that if you wanted to eliminate dengue, it was going to have to be by some other way."[31]

So while this Tahija Foundation–based initiative failed to achieve its main scientific objective—to reduce dengue infections—these community engagement efforts had important positive side effects in the fight against dengue. These included a better overall understanding of how to prevent dengue through community members' own actions, increased community ownership over mosquito management, and improved cross-sector partnerships, which brought more key stakeholders into the decision-making processes.

In addition, though the stakeholders did not know it at the time, this "failed" experiment built a solid foundation of trust and resilient networks in Yogyakarta. The relationships and experiences would be critical in laying the groundwork for another ambitious plan to eliminate dengue in which the Tahija family and foundation would be involved soon after.

The Tahija family was certainly pleased with the benefits that the community received from the study overall, but they were disappointed that it did not result in putting a big dent in dengue fever infections. And it took them seven years of effort and resources to figure that out. They had some thinking to do. Should they focus their foundation's resources on another long-term, resource-intensive experiment that may fail yet again to meet its core purpose of eradicating dengue, or should they focus on some other pressing philanthropic issue?

Often the end of one initiative kicks off the beginning of a new opportunity. Soon after the disappointing Sumilarv project results emerged, Dr. Duane Gubler approached Sjakon. Gubler was a world-renowned expert on insect-borne infectious diseases who had advised the Tahija family and foundation during the project. Gubler talked to Sjakon about how they now had significant infrastructure and knowledge for tackling dengue fever in Yogyakarta, and that they should consider alternative methods for eliminating dengue fever rather than focus their energy on other (potentially easier) philanthropic endeavors. Gubler then introduced Sjakon to the idea of working with an Australian research team led by Dr. Scott O'Neill, who had a promising new technique against dengue. That technique involved a novel way to infect mosquito larvae with a naturally occurring bacteria that seemed to stop mosquitoes from infecting people with the dengue virus. Would they be interested in talking to O'Neill about the possibility of working together on an innovative solution to eliminate dengue in Indonesia?

3

THE NEW MOSQUITOES

D r. Warsito Tantowijoyo clutched a nondescript container as if it contained the royal jewelry of the sultan of Yogyakarta while trying to sleep on a bench in Jakarta's Soekarno-Hatta International Airport—not knowing if he would be allowed back into his country. He may have been forgiven for seriously doubting why he ever agreed to quit his cushier and prestigious job at the Indonesian Science Institute to work for the Tahija Foundation as its lead entomologist on a new, leading-edge, but much more uncertain research project to eliminate dengue fever in Indonesia.

His latest adventure, which found him at this undesirable junction, felt like a mission impossible movie, but—unlike in a movie—he wasn't sure how it would end for the protagonists. He had rare and precious cargo that he alone was responsible for, which had to be transported safely across international borders. This cargo was also of international importance wrapped up in international intrigue!

However, if a stranger had somehow managed to break Warsito's iron grip on the container and open it, they likely would not have appreciated how valuable the contents were and may have, in fact, immediately dumped the contents in disgust after discovering what they were: mosquitoes and mosquito eggs. But these were no ordinary mosquitoes. These were highly prized and exceedingly rare laboratory mosquitoes that had a special mission—even if the mosquitoes themselves didn't know it.

Warsito's international mission-impossible-esque trek had started in Indonesia less than forty-eight hours earlier. After Indonesian officials had given him the green light to retrieve the valuable cargo from Melbourne, Australia, he had taken a red-eye flight from Indonesia. Landing in Melbourne that morning, not having gotten a good night's sleep, he was told by his Australian scientist counterparts that he would have to wait hours while the mosquito babies hatched. They were not cooperating with his timeline and would not be rushed. So, he checked into a nearby hotel to rest while he waited anxiously for his cargo. He had planned to fly back to Yogyarkarta that day, so he had little time to spare. With the clock ticking, an entourage of scientists delicately carrying a nondescript container arrived at the hotel as if they were escorting a king or queen.

This relay race against time had begun! These mosquitoes and eggs had to make it to his team's laboratory in Yogyakarta as quickly as possible, and they had to be kept alive. He rushed to the airport to make his flight—just in time. He would not let this cargo out of his sight and insisted that he hold it in his lap the entire flight while receiving plenty of curious gazes from fellow travelers, who likely wondered what this man was holding that was so important or if he were even entirely sane. He had made it to Indonesia. Unfortunately, any excitement from this achievement was short-lived: airport officials at Ngurah Rai International Airport (Denpasar) in Bali, Indonesia, refused to let him in with his mosquitoes, and they did not have the proper authority to provide him with a quarantine clearance permit. Instead, they recommended that he fly to Jakarta, where officials with the right level of authority could handle his case. What he was not told was that the office that would—hopefully—grant him the necessary permissions to enter the country with the mosquitoes was . . . closed until the next morning.

And why were these mosquitoes so precious and worth all this effort?

MICROBIAL WARFARE: USING BACTERIA TO FIGHT A VIRUS

Ever heard of a bacterium called *Wolbachia*? It is a surprisingly common bacterium estimated to occur naturally in over half of all known insect species. It was discovered in 1924 living within a "common house mosquito, *Culex pipiens*."[1]

Decades of scientific study of this bacterium following its discovery had concluded that *Wolbachia* bacteria are part of a genus of intracellular bacteria (i.e., live within host cells) that naturally occur in insect and arthropod species throughout the world. In fact, *Wolbachia* is so successful at infecting insects that an estimated 65-plus percent of insect species have it, making it the "most abundant intracellular bacteria genus" yet discovered.[2] In infecting a host, various *Wolbachia* strains have developed numerous ways to transmit themselves by altering the way in which the host reproduces offspring—and its approach often varies depending on the type of host.[3]

These innovative ways of altering host reproduction help explain why *Wolbachia* bacteria is so widespread. In mosquitoes, its infection methods are highly effective; *Wolbachia* can quickly infect an entire local population in only a few generations. One way it does this in mosquitoes is through what is called "cytoplasmic incompatibility" (CI). This biological process refers to whether or not mosquitoes will produce viable offspring based on their *Wolbachia* infection status. Either the offspring will be infected, or it won't hatch.

Dr. Scott O'Neill, director of the World Mosquito Program (WMP)[4] and a faculty member at Monash University in Melbourne, had begun studying the potential for *Wolbachia* to be used as a weapon in the fight against dengue in 1980. He started experimenting on fruit flies, which make nice test subjects because they are inexpensive to raise in a lab; they have extremely fast reproductive cycles (eight to fourteen days); and their genes—and the genes responsible for causing diseases in humans—are closely related to those of humans. In addition, they have been used so frequently as lab subjects that much of their biology is now well understood.[5] However, not until the late 1990s was a strain of *Wolbachia* (nicknamed "popcorn" for its appearance) identified that reproduced quickly in fruit flies and killed its host. Could this particular strain be introduced into the dengue-infected mosquito species to kill them before they could infect humans? It was worth a shot.

Even though *Wolbachia* was first identified in a mosquito species, it was never known to naturally infect *Ae. Aegypti*. Focusing their efforts on this primary dengue vector, O'Neill and his team had to find a way to introduce the *Wolbachia* popcorn strain into *Ae. Aegypti* mosquitoes. They decided the most viable method would be to infect mosquito eggs in their lab. That was much easier said than done. It took many years and thousands of painstaking egg injection attempts using a needle and human hand before one of O'Neill's students was finally successful in 2006. Unfortunately, the elation from this success was short-lived, as the popcorn strain was ultimately far too successful at killing the mosquito too quickly. The scientists realized this approach would not work in natural settings because these *Wolbachia*-infected mosquitoes would never have enough time to reproduce with the non-*Wolbachia*-infected population before they died.

Fortunately, a couple years later, in 2008, the researchers discovered that *Wolbachia* prohibited many viruses from growing in their mosquito host, including dengue (and other menacing viruses, such as chikungunya, yellow fever, and Zika). This meant that *Wolbachia* would not need to be developed as a weapon to kill mosquitoes; instead, it could be used to ultimately kill off viruses that lived in mosquitoes. And *Wolbachia*'s cytoplasmic incompatibility property could be used to quickly spread this virus-negating bacteria within populations of *Ae. Aegypti*. The team just had to reverse course and identify a *Wolbachia* strain that was not lethal (like popcorn) to its mosquito hosts. The particular *Wolbachia* strain they found that matched their new criteria was called "*w*Mel.

Now that O'Neill and his colleagues were able to produce *Wolbachia*-infected *Ae. Aegypti* mosquitoes in the lab that lived and could reproduce with wild mosquitoes, they had to find a suitable location for pilot studies. In 2011, he decided to conduct field studies in his own backyard—figuratively speaking—in Cairns, Australia (a city in Queensland, more than twenty-five hundred kilometers from the university, which is located in Victoria). Dengue infections from *Ae. Aegypti* also occurred in that area of Australia, so it would be beneficial to the human population there if the study was successful.

In the suburbs of Cairns, O'Neill's team collaborated with teams from other leading Australian universities to test their virus-blocking strategy. They started in early January 2011 using field study procedures that were intensive and involved a lot of moving parts, not least of which was convincing enough volunteers to be bitten by female mosquitoes so those mosquitoes would lay eggs for the researchers to collect. The team wanted to see if they could get wMel-infected mosquitoes not only to reproduce with wild non-wMel-infected mosquitoes but—through *Wolbachia's* cytoplasmic incompatibility property—to produce even more wMel-carrying wild mosquitoes in each subsequent generation. That in turn should reduce dengue infections given wMel's virus-blocking characteristic.[6]

After periodically releasing new batches of the wMel-infected mosquitoes in designated areas, every two weeks, O'Neill and his team monitored how many mosquitoes in the study areas they trapped that were carrying the *Wolbachia* strain. They stopped releasing in areas once the presence of Wolbachia was found in over 70 percent of the mosquitoes. They kept up the weekly releases as needed and continued the semiweekly monitoring regimen assiduously for approximately four months, taking a week off only when a powerful cyclone swept through the area in February.

It is important to note that the real work for the field study started well before January 2011. The scientists did not simply show up unannounced to release tens of thousands of mosquitoes in a populated area. Prior to the expected mosquito release phase of the study, the research teams spent two years meaningfully engaging the local communities through public meetings, one-on-one meetings, and thorough engagement with existing community groups. They used multiple tactics to uncover community concerns so they could respond via communication materials and, based on community feedback, adjust their experimental design. It was clear that they were actively listening to community concerns, and the community responded positively in turn. Random surveys to gauge study support had very high return rates, over 85 percent. And when the time came to release mosquitoes, only 3 percent of the households in the designated release areas declined to participate.

When they were able to analyze the data, O'Neill and his team were very pleased to confirm that *Wolbachia* could be established in a wild population. In fact, months later, nearly all the mosquitoes in study areas were *Wolbachia*-infected.

This pilot study in Cairns was seen as a success, but would this dengue virus suppression technique work on a much larger scale, such as in an entire city? The World Mosquito Program,[7] a not-for-profit organization dedicated to protecting the world from mosquito-borne diseases, decided to see if it was possible by undertaking a more ambitious *Wolbachia*-infected mosquito release project in Townsville, Australia, starting in 2013. Their main goals were to determine whether a large-scale deployment of *Wolbachia* was possible, and, if so, whether it could be done in a timely and efficient manner, in a way that was acceptable to communities.

This study ended up being an unmitigated success. O'Neill and his team believed their new *Wolbachia* technique for eliminating dengue infections could change the world for the better, but they needed to find allies to scale up this intervention in the field and have it succeed across multiple locations. WMP was being supported by funding from the Bill and Melinda Gates Foundation from nearly the beginning of the program. The foundation and other organizations had also supported WMP's Australian *Wolbachia* trials. However, to take it to the next level, they searched for a strong partner to help them attempt the intervention in non-Australian locations. It would be important to test the *Wolbachia* technique in a locale where dengue was endemic (i.e., regularly occurring and widespread), since it was not considered endemic to Australia. And as seems to be the case throughout this story, knowing the right people at the right time and the right place mattered. Just as O'Neill was starting trials in Australia to see how well this technology worked in the field, the Tahija Foundation's Sumilarv project was finishing up in Indonesia. As it turns out, the Tahijas and O'Neill both knew someone who wanted them to meet. This person was Duane Gubler.

AN AMERICAN MATCHMAKER

Now an emeritus professor at Duke-NUS Medical School, Gubler is a pioneer in dengue fever research. He has been studying this and other tropical infectious diseases for decades and is arguably the preeminent international expert on all things dengue. Over his career, he has published more than three hundred fifty papers on dengue fever and related topics.[8]

Gubler knew about O'Neill and his promising *Wolbachia* technology research in Australia. He knew the Tahija family and their keen interest in eliminating dengue in Indonesia. He had worked with the latter on the Sumilarv project and was instrumental in convincing the Tahijas to continue their efforts to eradicate dengue fever in Indonesia, as they had built up all this capacity and infrastructure for doing so. And he told O'Neill about the interest of the Tahijas in working to eliminate dengue. He thought that the Tahijas and O'Neill and his team would do well to at least meet each other to discuss how they might work together to deal with dengue.

Through Gubler, Sjakon Tahija and O'Neill first met in late 2010 in Yogyakarta, soon after the Tahijas learned about the disappointing results of their first dengue elimination project. Sjakon was presenting these results at a conference in Yogyakarta, when he met O'Neill, who was in attendance. Dr. Peter Ryan, a leading entomologist with WMP, also made a visit to the Tahija Foundation office to describe their new *Wolbachia* technique for eradicating dengue fever. When Ryan visited, the WMP team had not yet conducted any field studies in Australia, but he explained their technology and hopes for the study. After one of these initial meetings between the Tahija Foundation and WMP Global members, Sjakon wrote a succinct but upbeat note: "*Wolbachia* promises to eliminate dengue."[9]

While initial meetings with O'Neill and members of his WMP team out of Monash University were promising, the Tahijas had been exploring other viable options. Gubler had also introduced the Tahijas to another research team out of the University of Oxford in the United Kingdom that had a different approach to eliminating dengue fever. Theirs was a method designed by Dr. Luke Alphey and spun off as a commercialized product sold by Oxitec Ltd. starting in 2002.[10] Their principal scientific approach to eliminating dengue was to produce and release large numbers of sterilized male mosquitoes into the wild. These sterilized males would mate with wild females. It was expected that the reduction or eradication of mosquitoes (dengue-infected and otherwise) from this method would reduce dengue fever infections. The basic premise was that fewer (or no) mosquitoes would equate to fewer (or no) dengue infections.

When comparing the two new scientific approaches to eradicating dengue fever, Sjakon and the Tahija Foundation found O'Neill's approach much more attractive. One reason was that the Oxford option would require periodic shipments of large numbers of sterilized male mosquitoes from the UK with no clear project end date. It was unclear as to when, or even if, the entire dengue-infected mosquito population would be eradicated. The UK approach had worked on fruit flies in the United States, but would it really work on mosquitoes in Indonesia? And when a project does not have a clear end date, there is a greater likelihood that those involved would leave the venture before key objectives were met.

In contrast, WMP's *Wolbachia* technology had clearer expectations and a concrete end date for involvement by the Tahija Foundation and community. As WMP Global researcher Professor Cameron Simmons put it,

> I think the beauty of *Wolbachia* is that you don't rely on behavior changes to achieve good public health outcomes. Most things in life need community behavior changes for things to work, whether it is a smoking, obesity, or vaccine program that still require behavior changes. The beauty of the *Wolbachia* method is you do it at once so you will have sort of pulse of activities, but then the *Wolbachia* will stay within the mosquitoes. That is quite remarkable within the infectious disease landscape. . . . Here, we are talking about a level of the city or a country and in public health infectious diseases; the best approach was always prevention not treatment. . . . It is about stopping people from getting dengue altogether.[11]

Another aspect that favored the *Wolbachia* solution was that the Tahijas were sensitive to the perception of Indonesians as "guinea pigs" for new scientific experiments by foreign researchers, especially when those experiments may involve genetically modified insects. Genetically modifying organisms can invite controversy, and the Tahijas did not want controversy. In this case the technology and experiments already would have been done with Caucasian Australian citizens. This fact could go a long way toward reducing the potential perception by Westerners that Indonesians would be treated as guinea pigs. One more reason was that the Tahija family had an affinity for Australian culture and its people. Jean Tahija always made sure her husband and children traveled frequently to Australia for vacation and to visit their relatives to maintain and strengthen familial and intercultural relationships. These types of strong intercultural connections can be very important for resilient long-term partnerships, and the Tahija family members also took that into account when making their final decision.

Over the Sumilarv project years, the Tahija family had evolved a sophisticated way of thinking about the Tahija Foundation. For a while they had kept their family business operations and philanthropic organization separated conceptually and operationally. In one area were the Tahija family business management practices, and in another were the Tahija Foundation management practices. Each arm had seemingly very different purposes and operations. But this divide between business management and philanthropy management practices dissolved over time as the Tahijas began to see the value of business practices and management techniques that could be applied to improve their philanthropic endeavors. It was not a big leap, as they are proponents of the importance of considering all stakeholders when conducting their for-profit enterprises. Social goals are inherently part of, and make sense for, their business. Ultimately, they transformed the ethos and practices of the nonprofit Tahija Foundation into what is called "venture philanthropy," with the hope that they could fund social causes that had a positive transformative impact for Indonesians.

What is venture philanthropy? The traditional approach taken by many philanthropic organizations is to dole out funds for humanitarian causes but have little involvement in managing or tracking the output or outcomes from these funding initiatives. That is how the Tahija Foundation started approaching its management style and operations—as a more traditional philanthropic organization whose focus was more on funding humanitarian projects and less on managing or tracking an initiative's performance and impact.

That philanthropic approach changed over time. From the Tahijas' own business experiences, they found that venture capital (VC) firms adopted business practices that could help the Tahija Foundation improve the chances for higher social returns from their investments. VC investors focus their energy on new or entrepreneurial opportunities that promise high returns on their investment dollars. They are most interested in helping entrepreneurs grow their businesses. While these types of investments have a lot of upside potential (possibly exponential), the downside is that they are by nature very risky because there is a distinct chance of failure. By comparison, this type of financial commitment is much riskier (and/or much more uncertain regarding future returns) than buying stock in a Fortune 500 company that has decades of demonstrable financial success behind it.

To mitigate these higher investment risks, VC investors work closely with their investees (e.g., entrepreneurs) over the life of the investment to fund these nascent businesses. They share their wealth of business expertise from previous successful projects with entrepreneurs to help the business grow quickly.

Similar to VC investing, venture philanthropy (VP) investing is much more involved than simply providing funds to an organization. The VP investor is looking for new social investment projects that require a higher commitment from the investor (e.g., staff expertise) but whose potential social returns (e.g., outcomes) could be much higher than lower-risk alternatives.

Venture philanthropy is not for the faint of heart or for those who want to take a hands-off approach to their social investments or charitable giving. One critical aspect of venture capital management practices that applies to VP is that the funders are typically very involved in the entire process. High engagement means a lot of "sweat equity"; that is, a significant amount of involvement from investors working with the funded organizations, including managing the investments, monitoring benchmarks, and recommending new strategies to ensure that their charitable investments receive the highest social returns. Venture philanthropy made sense to the Tahijas before they knew there was a name for it.

Another key aspect of the Tahija Foundation's VP model is that the organization "intentionally takes on the risks of early and experimental endeavors with a vision that any positive outcomes of the ventures can be picked up or adopted by other organizations, the community or the government and develop them further to become a mainstream practice or initiative."[12] For the foundation's leadership, it was more than simply identifying those opportunities favored for high-impact social outcomes; these investment opportunities were also selected and developed with the express intent of making it easy for other interested parties to leverage what the foundation and its partners learned after the project was completed. They would track everything learned through a knowledge management team so that successful outcomes—and the processes that produced them—would not be proprietary (or simply forgotten) but intentionally designed and tracked so that other like-minded organizations could scale positive impact quickly.

The Tahijas had learned from the Sumilarv experience that they needed to take a different and more direct approach to the *Wolbachia* project. They knew they had to take a more active role in the project, helping to lead it rather than merely funding it. Sjakon Tahija says, "We learned some valuable lessons during the first failed project. There was a serious lack of leadership."[13]

Sjakon wanted to go ahead with the *Wolbachia* project, but he was hesitant to involve the rest of the family. He approached George about his plan to fund a dengue eradication project with O'Neill's WMP Global team. Sjakon thought they had a good chance of succeeding with the *Wolbachia* technique, but he still felt badly that the last dengue eradication project had not worked and did not want to drag George and his portion of the family's philanthropy money into yet another project that might fail. But George told him they should do it together. Sjakon said,

> With WMP Yogya we knew we were taking a risk; however, the impact if it was successful would revolutionize the management of viral diseases spread by the *Ae. aegypti* mosquito. With WMP the lead scientist was clearly capable and had proven that his methodology worked in Australia. I was hesitant to ask George and Laurel to jointly fund this study; however, they decided to take the risk. George insisted that management techniques used in business also be applied in the WMP Yogya. Scientists had to present clear milestones which they had to achieve if they were funded. The Tahija Foundation played a crucial role and was heavily involved in managing the study.[14]

George said that the fact that the family was united was very important, and Shelly affirmed that while family discussions were not easy, they needed to tackle the project together. "We considered many things, including the responsibilities of the lead investigator and his team, as well as the visits and talks we had with the EDP [Eliminate Dengue Project] team at Monash. We also understood that this project was not without risk."[15]

Laurel and George both trusted Sjakon and Shelly's scientific judgment. Laurel said, "I think it was implicit in our combined vision to learn from past mistakes, build on what the foundation had already invested in the community network, and over-come the challenges."[16] George added, "Having a large reserve of mutual trust among G2 [the second generation and Family Council] had a crucial role in improving the odds of success when we embarked on this new and unknown journey. In the few cases where there is family synergy, families can be uniquely qualified to take on long-term risks. In our case the unified stand of the Family Council provided confidence to our project cham-pions to overcome some incredible odds. We are very conscious of having a unified front."[17]

In addition, the family decided that they would underwrite the expenses for the Yogya project. This gave them more control and enabled the foundation to more actively manage the project, including hiring many of the key people. Of course, they worked cooperatively with WMP, but they were able to be responsive to the local conditions in Indonesia and Yogyakarta since they were so familiar with the people, stakeholders, and culture. The failed Sumilarv project gave them a big head start on what was needed if the *Wolbachia* project was to be successful.

Much of this background begins to explain why Dr. War-sito Tantowijoyo found himself desperately trying to sleep on an uncomfortable airport bench while never letting go of his dear mosquito container, the cause of all his recent challenges. Inside Warsito's tightly held container, adult mosquitoes blithely buzzed about while mosquito larvae waited to hatch, no doubt not appreciating their critical role in this story. They likely also didn't know they were the result of years of intricately complex (and painstakingly precise) scientific laboratory work conducted by O'Neill and his team, who had been perfecting a microin-jection technique to insert the *Wolbachia* bacteria into mosquito eggs so that, as adults, the mosquitoes would be infected with *Wolbachia*.

Warsito and his mosquitoes were so close to their final destination. "No pain, no gain," was his motto, but after all the pain he had experienced in the prior forty-eight hours, would he be allowed into Indonesia or would all of these painstaking plans and efforts be for nothing?

Fortunately, he awoke the next morning in the airport to discover that he and his container of mosquitoes would be allowed to enter the country. These "royal babies"—as lab staff began calling them—would end up being the ancestors of countless mosquitoes now buzzing around the Yogyakarta region.

A huge factor in securing his successful reentry into his country was the faculty and staff at the University of Gadjah Mada in Yogyakarta. They worked diligently with Indonesian officials throughout Warsito's airport travails to ensure that he had the right clearance permissions to enter the country. And why might faculty and staff from the University of Gadjah Mada expend so much effort to help Dr. Tantowijoyo, who worked for the WMP Yogyakarta team, which was funded by the Tahija Foundation?[18] Because the university had recently joined WMPY in a long-term strategic partnership with the Tahija Foundation and the WMP Global team.

4

THE PARTNERSHIP

THE AUSTRALIAN CONNECTION

About a year before the University of Gadjah Mada (UGM) joined the WMPY strategic partnership, the Tahijas' and Scott O'Neill's WMP Global team continued to discuss a possible partnership after their initial meetings had gone so well. In early 2011, Sjakon Tahija, Shelley Tahija, and Tahija Foundation team members flew to Queensland to meet O'Neill and the WMP Global team. There, the two groups continued to explore the feasibility of WMP's *Wolbachia* technology intervention in an Indonesia setting. The Tahija Foundation representatives introduced themselves at WMP's annual meeting and observed O'Neill's and WMP Global's field study testing the feasibility of releasing *Wolbachia*-infected mosquitoes into densely populated areas. The Tahijas enjoyed seeing the mosquito laboratory and visiting the neighborhoods in Cairns to watch the release of study mosquitoes (and help release some themselves) in Australian neighborhoods.

This trip essentially sealed the deal for the Tahijas, and they made the decision to seek a formal partnership agreement with the Australians. The progress of the study in Australia looked promising, but the Tahija family and foundation leadership knew that Australian scientists conducting a study in their own country with Australian-designed technology and local mosquitoes with local citizens' consent and Australian governmental backing was one thing. Trying to do the same thing in Indonesia was going to be much more difficult. As the Tahijas' and O'Neill's WMP Global team began to sketch out an audacious long-term plan to test whether the new *Wolbachia* technique could eliminate dengue fever in Indonesia, they knew they would need a skilled and trustworthy local Indonesian partner to help navigate complex governmental and cultural issues in Indonesia.

For one thing, the national governments of Australia and Indonesia had not always agreed with or trusted each other during their decades-long relationship.[1] In 2013, a scandal erupted when documents were leaked revealing that Australian government spies had been attempting to listen in on private phone calls of the Indonesian president, Susilo Bambang Yudhoyono, and several of his close family members as far back as 2009.[2] Add to these geopolitical sensitivities the difficult language barriers and stark cultural differences between the two countries; for example, in terms of religious affiliations, the vast majority of Indonesians identify as Muslim, while the majority of Australians identify as Christian. To top it all off, Indonesian government officials were often leery of foreign-based scientific studies because of previous instances of international researchers exploiting Indonesia's flora, fauna, artifacts, and people in the name of science.

YOGYAKARTA AND THE UNIVERSITY OF GADJA MADA

The Tahijas already had experience with a field study in Yogyakarta and a strong foundation built with stakeholders in that area based on their Sumilarv project, so they felt they had a good location for an Indonesian study. But they knew they needed another local partner to develop and implement a long-term, high-quality, and large-scale field study. It had to be a local partner they could trust, one that had a good reputation with local communities and many of the requisite skill sets available to conduct leading-edge science, that could build additional staff and infrastructure capacities necessary for the project (with help from the Tahija Foundation and WMP Global), and could help navigate Indonesia's complex bureaucratic and cultural landscape.

Ultimately, UGM rose to the top as the strongest potential strategic partner. UGM researchers had been involved in the Sumilarv project, and the institution had a strong reputation in the Yogyakarta region.

Long-term partnerships can be powerful catalysts for solving societal issues, but they also take a lot of work. At their best, they can unite the varied strengths of participating organizations to create innovative, comprehensive, and sustainable solutions that a single organization could not do alone. At their worst, they can devolve into fractious and acrimonious affairs that waste resources and burn bridges across sectors. They can be fraught with confusion and friction as organizational stakeholders from very different backgrounds and motivations team up, perhaps for the first time, to agree on common goals and strategies to solve seemingly intractable problems. These multistakeholder partnerships also may be the only effective way to solve grand challenges that adversely affect social issues, such as trying to eliminate dengue fever forever for the benefit of millions of people from all walks of life.

The Tahija Foundation's chief executive officer at the time, Anastasius Wahyuhadi, who was instrumental in securing this partnership during intense negotiations, discussed the reasoning behind asking UGM to be a partner institution and the difficulties they knew they would face with an international collaboration.

> The Tahija Foundation finally selected UGM's Faculty of Medicine to become its Indonesian partner and research executor of the *Wolbachia* project. After the Sumilarv project ended, the Tahija Foundation still possessed adequate project infrastructures and human resources at UGM, who were ready to start working with the new project. The Tahija Foundation fully realized that setting up a multiparty research project was massive work. The key is to choose rightful and trustful partners. This collaboration involving Australian and Indonesian scientists might likely present astonishing challenges, such as how and what contributions they should share; different cultural background is another tricky issue and perhaps personal clashes might occur during the course of the project.[3]

UGM had a rich history in the Yogyakarta region. It was formally established as a public institution of higher education by the newly independent Indonesian government in 1949.[4] Its namesake, Gadjah Mada, was a fourteenth-century prime minister for the Majapahit Empire celebrated as a national hero for unifying much of the Indonesian archipelago.[5] Since its founding, UGM has grown to have a significant presence in local communities. Each year thousands of faculty members have taught tens of thousands of students, granting a broad range of undergraduate, professional, and graduate degrees from over two hundred study programs. In addition, within its core mission is the promise to "carry out education, research and community service."[6] With community service as a core value, its staff and students frequently have been involved in local community-based projects and research. The experience and local social capital that UGM could bring to the table would be crucial for the planned Indonesian implementation of a *Wolbachia* technology study. The Tahija Foundation and WMP Global were confident that UGM had the capacity, expertise, and values they were seeking in a strong strategic partner. But would UGM accept their offer to join them in trying this innovative new approach to eliminate dengue fever?

Given the nature of the study and expertise required, the partners reached out to university leadership at UGM's Faculty of Medicine and Public Health. The WMPY project's three key internal stakeholder organizations then became the World Mosquito Program Global team at Monash University, UGM, and the Tahija Foundation. They needed to develop a mutually agreed-upon understanding to get this complex, long-term project off the ground. The Tahija Foundation leadership knew that this type of research project would be arduous; trusting and trustworthy partners were needed for this extensive commitment with the audacious goal of eliminating dengue fever where others (including themselves) had failed before. They had found prospective partner institutions that fit the bill, but they also knew that bringing together experts from other countries to take on this long-term, multiphase project would need a strong foundation of trust. Indeed, when the UGM leadership read the original memorandum of understanding (MoU) designed by the Tahija Foundation and WMP Global, they refused to sign it. There was more work to be done among the three partners.

Tahija Foundation leaders were interested in funding, managing, and supporting much of the project, but they were not interested in the intellectual property benefits that could result from what was discovered and developed with the deployment of the *Wolbachia* technology in Indonesia. UGM, however, had a different perspective on the project.

UGM leaders saw this strategic collaboration and research opportunity as having great potential.[7] Nongovernment research funding was more highly coveted than government funding but was hard to find. By comparison, the Tahija Foundation's funding model involved multiyear time horizons for studies with far fewer bureaucratic reporting expectations. That was highly appealing to UGM. Another benefit would be that UGM researchers could build up their scientific network by collaborating with foreign experts, which could boost their self-confidence and access to other world-class experts for future success. For the UGM researchers, this arrangement provided a healthy balance of academic and practical relevance.

Despite these advantages, UGM was were not ready to sign the MoU as written, for two reasons. There was a concern about the ethical and reputational risks involved with such a new technology, and UGM had to consider intellectual property (IP) issues. On the ethical risk, UGM researchers reached out to their network in Thailand, who at that time had declined to adopt the technology due to security concerns. UGM leadership also had to consider the consequences if the long-term, large-scale, and highly visible project failed. Failure after devoting years of resource-intensive efforts to the project could damage the university's reputation. Alternatively, a successful partnership and project could boost UGM's reputation as a world-class university that made significant headway against a lingering public health issue.

Intellectual property rights issues included concerns around scientific publications, inventions, and patents. In the original proposal, WMP Global claimed all intellectual property rights that would result from the research. Tahija Foundation leadership was fine with that, since such rights were not why they were funding the research. However, UGM felt that since its scientists and academics would be heavily involved in the research process, they should get some credit for their critical contributions. In addition, having UGM researchers as lead corresponding authors (first author) on intellectual property products (e.g., academic journal publications) would be important for their career advancement. In sum, UGM leaders wanted to be treated as equal IP partners with WMP researchers.

Finally, in September 2011, after months of intense negotiations, a new MoU was cosigned by Tahija Foundation, the World Mosquito Program Global at Monash University, and the University of Gadjah Mada. Monash University would not claim all IP rights; instead, UGM and Monash University researchers would be co-owners of all intellectual property that resulted from the research. All the other details were hammered out, with the understanding that terms could change during the project if the partners thought that was necessary. In fact, some renegotiations did occur over the life of the project, but none was nearly as contentious as the one regarding IP rights.

WORKING TOGETHER

The partners began the critically important work of designing a feasible and rigorous research plan for the new initiative, called the World Mosquito Program—Yogyakarta (WMPY). The Tahija family realized this was a risky project. As Wayhyuhadi commented, "The possibility of its failure was as high as the Sumilarv project. But the family kept moving forward to stay positive and to remain very hopeful that the *Wolbachia* project would yield major results for the good of the people. . . . We did not know whether the project was viable. This project might contain potential risks and challenges."[8]

Trust and respect are very important concepts in Indonesia. They represent a form of social currency that can help explain why some relationships succeed and others fail. They can be the glue that keeps individuals and organizations working together when adverse events invariably arise. Building trust and showing respect to people and organizations takes considerable effort, empathy, and intentionality. Many members of the WMPY project team talked about feeling comfortable with their colleagues, many of whom became like family. And it is not as though family members do not have conflicts; it is just that they often find ways to fight and get mad at each other but still coexist and work together to accomplish common goals. Some long days were put in by team members at various phases of the project and plenty of stressful situations. But they began to truly trust and respect one another, which kept them going during tough times.

Trust among the strategic partner organizations was also paramount. Intrepid explorers, entrepreneurs, and scientists would likely agree that the road is frequently bumpy when you are blazing new trails. However, when partners and teammates have built a strong foundation of trust, they are more resilient when they encounter the bumps and travails of the journey (e.g., interorganizational tension, intrateam conflict, and natural calamities). This partnership resiliency emerges from a strong base of trust. During this project, trust was built through frequent communication across teams and organizations, and differences were hashed out responsively and responsibly. The criticality of trust in a relationship and the importance of honesty and humility in dealing with others were key concepts that emerged from interviewing numerous stakeholders involved in the WMPY project.

Scott O'Neill put it this way:

> I think trust is easy when there is transparency. It is hard to trust someone when you can't see what is going on. . . . We have committed to having values of transparency, of honesty, and those values make trust easier. And the Tahija family has those values. They are very honest, transparent, and trustworthy, so it makes the collaboration easy so far. When you don't have those things, it will make the work harder. When motivations are clear, people understand, and then it will be easy to do something good. We have good interaction with the Tahija family and our UGM partner because of those values, those properties.[9]

In addition, having the right people serve as communicators builds strong bridges across teams and organizations, which was key to reducing friction and staying on track to meet project objectives when tensions invariably arose, especially when a project includes multicultural and multidisciplinary teams within a multistakeholder partnership. Excellent communication practices may be of the utmost importance when a large team of experts from across disciplines works together on a societal-level challenge.

From the Tahija Foundation's perspective, Wahyuhadi mentioned how the first two years of the project were challenging, with so-called nontechnical issues among the strategic partners being harder to deal with than the technical ones. Dealing with innovative new techniques and cutting-edge science was one thing, but dealing with interpersonal and interorganizational politics and disagreements with a small army of experts was a whole different beast. At the organizational level, Tahija Foundation leaders were well aware of these potential nontechnical stumbling blocks. One strategy for handling some of these concerns was taking the lead on negotiations but adopting an accommodating approach when working on the WMPY partnership agreement, to prevent ego from each party that could derail the project. They did not request any copyright ownership, for example, and wanted all project results to be shared freely for the benefit of other developing countries that may want to implement similar programs. Foundation leaders even emphasized that they were proactively looking out for the interests of the other parties whether or not those interests directly benefited the Tahija Foundation. This generous approach surprised the Tahija Enterprise's legal team, but it was consistent with the Tahija family's humanistic values and principles, which were made clear to staff during training sessions and interactions with them.[10]

Exceptional communication skills were needed to build a relationship of trust among the WMPY partners and with local government officials, and Tahija family members expressed their gratitude for the relationship-building and communication expertise that Wahyuhadi demonstrated. As Sjakon Tahija succinctly put it, "Wahyuhadi basically translated the family's wishes and carried them out in Yogya[karta] by communicating to the Gadjah Mada University and the provincial government. He worked hard to make sure there were no misunderstandings between the [Tahija Foundation], Gadjah Mada University, and the provincial government."[11] Laurel Tahija was also impressed by Wahyuhadi's communication skills, noting, "I find Pak Wahyu is a gifted communicator with a reflective background perhaps honed during his days of Jesuit education and candidacy for priesthood. I feel it is an honor to work with him."[12]

Another example of exemplary communication skills was exhibited by UGM's Dr. Adi Utarini—or Prof. Uut, as she was known—the principal investigator of the *Wolbachia* Research

Project. Several project members praised her as being adept at smoothing over many heated interunit disagreements when she was WMPY's project leader. She was in the challenging position of trying to coordinate the work of about one hundred scientists as well as communicate with multiple external stakeholder groups (e.g., government agencies, media, community members). With so much top talent recruited for the WMPY project, Prof. Uut often found herself acting not as a scientist utilizing her technical skills but, instead, employing excellent communication and facilitation skills when confronted with other talented scientists who got "involved in heated arguments and persistently defended their opinion" when decisions had to be made on the project.[13] In other words, experts fought (verbally) with one another and were often not happy to admit that others might be right—and Prof. Uut had to patiently referee those conflicts to defuse tense situations and keep the project moving forward. She said of such circumstances,

> I found that there were a number of strong and talented leaders in each unit. Often, they had to be involved in heated arguments and persistently defended their opinion. As the project's team leader and principal investigator, my job is to synchronize all units and to ensure the flow of work runs smoothly. . . . I realized that I had a pool of extraordinary and dedicated scientists on the team. Therefore, it was my responsibility to make this project successful by applying appropriate managerial and communication strategies. . . . Basically, I have been acting not only as a project leader and a principal investigator but also a glue that sticks everybody together. In addition, I am also a facilitator and a communicator who connects the three collaborators—UGM, the Tahija Foundation and WMP Global—with government agencies and other multistakeholders.[14]

Dr. Riris Andono Ahmad, one of the project scientists, said, "This is not solely about a scientific project done in laboratories. It deals with issues that affect the lives of thousands of people in target project areas. . . . Managing these complexities has never been easy. It required technical and managerial skills, communication ability, and, more importantly, a compassionate heart."[15]

Fostering an environment of trust and having the right people in the right positions for effective communication are critical when numerous teams and organizations are working together to meet project objectives. But other ingredients are needed as well: management and funding.

Understanding the WMPY project not only as a cutting-edge science experiment utilizing new technology but also as an expert entrepreneurial endeavor[16] helps explain how the project's original trio of partners had to forge new relationships and convince others to be cooperating stakeholders. The WMPY partners had to find ways to reach out to community members, government officials, and others to demonstrate that they shared common ground and that their involvement (or lack thereof) as stakeholders would affect the project's outcome. And a successful outcome from this endeavor could lead to immense value creation (financial and nonfinancial) for all stakeholder groups. Children would no longer die or become seriously ill from dengue fever. Employees would no longer miss work due to being ill or caring for sick loved ones. Public health officials would no longer have to worry about dengue fever outbreaks that frequently threatened to overwhelm hospitals.

The WMPY project would involve new technology, new mosquito-breeding processes, and new vector disbursement methods. The entomology team was able to receive advice from WMP Global scientists, but much had to be learned and developed by the Indonesian-based team on the frontier of scientific innovations. As an example, the WMPY entomology laboratory team lacked an exact formula (from WMP Global scientists or anyone else) for how many times they should crossbreed wild Indonesian mosquitoes with *Wolbachia*-infected Australia-based lab mosquitoes so the mosquitoes they released would have a similar level of resistance as wild Indonesian *Ae. Aegypti* mosquitoes against a widely used brand of insecticide called Baygon. This insecticide was used frequently in the local neighborhoods where the project would release its crossbred mosquitoes. If insecticide resistance was too low, too many mosquitoes would die from the insecticide when released in the field (probably invalidating the study), but if resistance was too high, residents and officials might be upset that too many mosquitoes had become immune to the insecticide. Just like the story of Goldilocks and the three bears, their project's crossbreeding design had to be just right. But the entomologists didn't have an exact formula for how to get it right because this experiment had never been tried before. (It turns out that the optimal number of times to crossbreed wild with captive mosquitoes was five.)[17]

During the ten-year project, there were enough discoveries like the one just described to fill another book. That didn't go unnoticed during. These just-in-time problem-solving discoveries generated a lot of new knowledge that the WMPY organization wanted to capture for future reference during the project as well as transfer to other interested implementers after the project's completion. To this end, the Tahijas insisted that a knowledge management (KM) team be formed in phase III (see later text for details about the phases). They understood that having learned so much from the Sumilarv failure, they wanted to document what was learned from the *Wolbachia* project. This would be especially important if the project succeeded and could be exported to other geographies.

MANAGING THE PROJECT
AT THE FOUNDATION

While the scientists worked through new scientific discoveries, disputes and misunderstandings occurred between the scientists and professional staff who held different administrative roles and responsibilities in the WMPY project. Those roles included financial professionals, data managers, knowledge management professionals, administrative assistants, which are common in nonprofit and for-profit organizations. The organizational structure created working relationships that many were unaccustomed to. For example, some scientists were not used to having to submit budget requests to financial professionals to buy the materials or attend the trainings they required for their work—and also sometimes having those requests denied.

Not surprisingly, misunderstandings and conflict occurred among these professionals. A general manager was needed to oversee and support project planning, management, budgeting, and procurement to meet timelines and stay within budget. Someone in this challenging position would need the right experience and communication skills. In 2016, the Tahija Foundation hired Widi Nugroho as WMPY's general manager. Nugroho had come out of retirement after almost thirty years at the Chevron oil company. In this new position, Nugroho described feeling like a "referee" and "peacekeeper" in a balancing act of supporting the scientists' work to ensure that all administrative and procurement activities were supported while meeting legal requirements.[18]

Buying and importing sophisticated equipment also complicated matters, requiring considerable procurement expertise and a surfeit of patience. For instance, Nugroho's team had to go through an Indonesian agency to buy materials from a

Swiss-based company. WMPY paid the invoice and then waited months for the badly needed laboratory materials to arrive. But the materials never arrived. The management team contacted the company, only to find out that it had gone bankrupt! Tahija Foundation finance department staff came to the rescue, demanding a refund from the bankrupt company. Nugroho's team got their money back.

Given the nature of this innovative project and their expertise in funding complex field studies, the Tahija Foundation and Tahija family had planned for and implemented their venture philanthropy funding and management model for this long-term project with their strategic partners. They relied on their strategic partners to handle the complex scientific aspects of the project while they focused on other important organizational activities related to funding and knowledge, human resources, and project management. Monash University also sent a finance manager to train UGM and WMPY staff on budgeting, planning, and project management related to funding large-scale research projects. That enabled the scientists to concentrate on their research while administrative professionals focused on supporting and accelerating their research. While this approach caused some consternation early on, the scientists were able to focus on conducting rigorous science. As one scientist put it, "I felt so relieved that we did not have to do those things [detailed financial and administrative work]. We have been focusing on scientific research and on producing the best evidence."[19] This was by design.

As the WMPY strategic partnership began to unfold, the Tahija Foundation brought to bear its business resources, human resource development capacity, as well as project management and governance expertise. UGM brought scientific leadership, local community engagement experience and a keen understanding of the local regulatory environment and how to advocate for the project. WMP Global brought and shared its scientific expertise regarding the *Wolbachia* technology, quality assurance processes, and access to a global network of experts. Together these complementary partners developed a four-phase, evidence-based project plan for implementation in the Yogyakarta region of Indonesia that was expected to take approximately ten years to complete.

The strategic partnership's long-term plan was based on a "phase-gate process," which breaks up a project into distinct go/no-go milestones. When a milestone is reached, the person or group with authority decides whether or not to continue with the project after evaluating its progress. If those in authority approve it, the project can continue to the next planned phase. In other words, it's a "go." If they don't think the project is meeting its objectives, or serious issues arise, it is discontinued ("no-go"). This approach gives funders opportunities for logical checkpoints in a long-term project when they can exit early if necessary, decreasing their risk of continuing to fund long-term projects that may have little to no chance of success.

As funders of the project, the Tahija Foundation board had to give final approval for the project to continue to the next phase. The WMPY project plan was separated into four main phases:

- Phase I: Safety & Feasibility (~2 years)
- Phase II: Small-Scale Release (~2 years)
- Phase III: Large-Scale Release (~4 years)
- Phase IV: Scale-Up (~1 year)

As mentioned, the entire project was expected to last a little over nine years. Perhaps not unexpectedly, it took a little longer than anticipated; the large-scale releases during phase III needed a year's extension (the team had not anticipated a global pandemic). Given the nature of a new scientific technology that was to be implemented, in which a community would bear the brunt of any unexpected adverse effects, the phases were designed to make public safety the top priority. To this end, Phase I involved studying the safety and feasibility of releasing *Wolbachia*-infected mosquitoes in Indonesia. The project leaders had to determine whether an Indonesian team could build the capacity, infrastructure, and expertise to release viable infected mosquitoes into designated local neighborhoods. Assuming the outcome was a "go," phase II would involve a small-scale field release of *Wolbachia*-infected mosquitoes in Yogyakarta-areaneighborhoods. (In business this may be called a "pilot," testing a concept before a full-scale release.) The researchers needed to build capacity and continue testing the feasibility of their ultimate goal—a large-scale release in a large section of a high-density urban area that might actually defeat dengue fever.

Phase III would be the equivalent of a crescendo in an orchestral arrangement, if all the researchers, managers, and support staff were musicians. (Many WMPY staff in fact were talented musicians, some were in music groups or bands outside of work. Staff mentioned that Dr. Utarini—an accomplished pianist—was so successful at leading the project, since she performed like a music conductor bringing harmony among the various teams.) If the third phase was successful, that meant the *Wolbachia* technology was effective at combating dengue fever. A "go" at the end of this phase would lead to phase IV, a scaling up of the phase III implementation techniques to cover the entire Yogyakarta region.

Throughout these phases, advisory boards and steering committees were formed for ethics oversight, technical assistance, and strategic management. The main steering committee comprised multiple leaders from all three partner organizations. A project leader and general manager reported directly to this committee and were responsible for overall project management and leadership.

Besides the Steering Committee, other stakeholders held advisory roles to assist project leaders on numerous aspects of the project, including technical and public health expertise. For example, a Yogyakarta-based public health institution, Dinas Kesehatan—Daerah Istimewa Yogyakarta, provided guidance to the Steering Community on local public health issues. Multidisciplinary experts were invited to be join the Board of Advisers, which was tapped for advice as needed. Technical advisers from Monash University, including Dr. Ari Hoffmann and Dr. Petrina Johnson, trained WMPY staff and UGM faculty on scientific, financial management, and project management activities.

The WMPY strategic partners were excited about their overall research plan and the science and management principles supporting it. They began to trust one another and their partnership's ability to successfully implement important scientific research in Indonesia. Now they just had to convince others outside their strategic partnership of the same.

5

MORE STAKEHOLDERS

D r. Adi Utarini was devastated. She was in a meeting at the Ministry of Research, Technology and Higher Education's Jakarta office. Around the room were Indonesian experts from a variety of disciplines, including some from the University of Indonesia and the Indonesian Institute of Science (LIPI), as well as high-ranking government officials from several agencies. The WMPY project had support from some of these officials, such as Dr. Sangkot Marzuki, former director of the Eijkman Institute for Molecular Biology and president of the Indonesian Academy of Sciences, who had been involved in earlier permit approvals needed for previous project phases. However, several others in attendance were skeptical.

Utarini was there to get their approval for a research permit for the WMPY project's third phase—the crucial phase that could provide them with the strongest scientific evidence that their solution could be scaled up to a large enough area to be an effective public health initiative for preventing dengue fever. She responded politely but firmly to yet another official who questioned her motivations related to bringing Australian-born mosquitoes into Indonesia for her research project. Why couldn't they just raise Indonesian mosquitoes and inject those with the

Wolbachia bacteria? Why couldn't Indonesian experts do all this on their own without Australian scientists?

But it wasn't that simple. They didn't have the expertise or infrastructure to easily start from scratch in Indonesia. That would delay the research project, be unnecessarily expensive, and miss an excellent opportunity for an international collaboration among world experts. Plus, it would be far more efficient and practical to import Australian-bred *Aedes aegypti* that were infected with *Wolbachia* bacteria from the WMP Global experts. Utarini also explained that WMP experts, led by Scott O'Neill, were reputable scientists who had spent many years perfecting the *Wolbachia* technology; they didn't have the luxury of starting from scratch in Indonesia. Indonesian scientists didn't have the resources or time to redo all this difficult work. Who was going to fund such expensive research? She tried to explain all this again as politely but firmly as she could.

Would their innovative and potentially groundbreaking research be rejected again because of strong risk aversion, fear, and nationalistic sentiments? What could she say to overcome the suspicions and concerns of so many authority figures in the room who had the power to scuttle her project? Tears started to well up.

COLLEGIAL SUPPORT

Utarini and her colleagues were experiencing the hard way how difficult stakeholder engagement can be.[1] She had not forgotten about prior attempts to secure government and academic approval for WMPY that had ended in momentary setbacks, so it was not surprising that she was so discouraged in this meeting. It seemed that roadblocks were always being put up for this project. Years earlier, two prominent Indonesian scientists, Dr. Sofia Mubarika Haryana and Dr. Yatie Soenarto, had also traveled to Jakarta when they first tried to get the necessary government permissions to bring mosquitoes in from Australia for WMPY's first phase of research.

Haryana, a professor and deputy dean in UGM's Faculty of Medicine and Public Health and an expert in histology (the study of tissues and their structures), was responsible for the school's external relations and collaborations. She had been asked by the dean, Dr. Ali Ghufron Mukti, to meet with the Tahija Foundation when UGM leaders was still deciding whether or not to join the partnership. She had worked previously with Shelley Tahija at the Indonesian Cancer Foundation, but she had not yet met Sjakon Tahija until a meeting to discuss the potential of WMP's *Wolbachia* technology to combat dengue fever.

Haryana was aware of the Tahija Foundation's previous work on the Sumilarv project, and even though it hadn't succeeded in meeting its scientific objectives to reduce dengue, she was impressed with the quality of the foundation's work and the energy the Tahija family consistently put into trying to solve Indonesia's dengue problem. This time the plan was to try the *Wolbachia* technology with an Australian-based partner, Scott O'Neill's World Mosquito Program at Monash University. She and a UGM team joined the Tahija Foundation's team to visit Australia to see how the *Wolbachia* technology was being implemented in northern Australia. There, O'Neill, and his team presented their novel approach to eliminate dengue via *Wolbachia*-infected mosquitoes. Their presentation was compelling—enough that when Haryana and her UGM colleagues returned to Indonesia, UGM leadership began detailed discussions on how best to structure a partnership as well as the Indonesian regulations and research logistics they would need to address. One of the first hurdles would be how to get their research approved by an Indonesian research ethics board.[2]

Haryana's colleague, Dr. Yatie Soenarto, is considered by many to be the "mother of modern paediatrics in Indonesia."[3] Soenarto is known for being instrumental in improving the lives, and reducing fatality rates, of countless Indonesian children through her epidemiological discoveries and innovations. A prolific instructor and researcher, Soenarto has taught generations of pediatricians over a career spanning four decades. And her influence goes well beyond Indonesia, as she developed effective treatments against severe diarrhea that have become a global standard and helped identify a rotavirus that is the primary cause of severe diarrhea around the world. Interested in international collaborations, she has worked frequently with the University of Melbourne on programs aimed at furthering world-class disease management research, including a joint effort that led to the development of a rotavirus vaccine.[4]

While Soenarto's main focus was on combating the harmful effects of diarrhea, she had also worked on other tropical diseases, including dengue. For children in Indonesia, dengue was the fifth most likely cause of death.[5] But there still was no effective dengue vaccine, and they had been stuck trying the same interventions against dengue for decades, to little effect. Soenarto was excited when she heard about a new intervention that might change all that. And when O'Neill invited her to visit his laboratory at Monash University so she could see for herself how they injected *Wolbachia* bacteria into mosquitoes and describe how the process could work to remove dengue from an area, she was amazed. She had never seen that type of research for mosquito-borne diseases and knew it could be beneficial for Indonesia given dengue's negative impact there.

Soenarto was no stranger to international and multisector partnerships, or the complex research approval processes and permits needed to conduct leading-edge research in Indonesia. She knew they had their work cut out for them to convince others that this was a partnership opportunity worth pursuing, one that could be a game changer in the fight against dengue in Indonesia. Soenarto thought it was important enough that she and Haryana "went everywhere, we knocked on everybody's door to beg" for their support of the project.[6]

Their diligence and perseverance ultimately paid off. Soenarto and Haryana were instrumental champions in gaining support from their UGM colleagues and Indonesian government officials in their networks in the early stages of what would become the WMPY project. But the road was rocky at times. These two distinguished scientists led the application process for a research permit from the National Ethical Commission and the University of Indonesia's Ethics Board. They then traveled to Jakarta to meet with those officials and others from the Ministry of Health to discuss their research plans for WMPY's first phase. The commission members questioned them relentlessly, raising concerns about the environmental risks and public safety concerns related to importing *Wolbachia*-infected mosquitoes from Australia. Ultimately, their application for a research permit was rejected.

Though these indefatigable women may have been discouraged, they were not defeated; they considered their options. They regrouped with the Tahija Foundation and UGM leadership. Since the research project was going to take place in Yogyakarta anyway and far from Jakarta, they decided that to try again with UGM's Ethics Board. And to reduce conflict-of-interest concerns, they included members of Indonesia's National Research Board, Ministry of Health officials, Yogyakarta Research Board members, and other prominent Indonesian scientists outside UGM. And this time they were successful. Their project was approved, but with a difficult-to-implement stipulation. The Ethics Board required that every adult family member living in a household would have to consent to research that involved allowing a bucketful of mosquito larvae to spawn into mosquitoes on their property—and even in their homes. Many Indonesians belong to large families with multiple generations living under one roof, and unless all family members consented, the researchers could not deploy the mosquito buckets at that household or anywhere within a radius of twenty to fifty meters.[7]

The WMPY team saw the ethical reasons behind why it was necessary to collect individual consent, given standard scientific protocols, but it was going to be much more difficult for them to accomplish their goal and could seriously erode the quality of their research if they experienced high levels of nonconsent. They had their work cut out for them. The team knew the reason they would be conducting their study in the Yogyakarta region was because of the Tahija Foundation's previous experience building up infrastructure for research there and UGM's strong presence and reputation locally. However, the team also realized that they needed to use all the tools in their toolkit to improve their chances of gaining sufficient community member consent to conduct scientifically rigorous field studies. Consent rates and community support had to be as close to 100 percent as possible; the researchers needed someone whom the local community in the Yogyakarta region looked up to, someone who would champion their cause. They also needed to make sure the local government authorities would permit them to conduct their rather unorthodox and large-scale study. Fortunately, they found someone who had the necessary strengths: Sri Sultan Hamengkubuwono X.

THE SULTAN

You could forgive Tahija Foundation CEO Anastasius Wahyu-hadi for feeling anxious as he waited for one of the most important meetings of his life. One wonders how much of the splendor of the sultan's palace of Yogyakarta (also known as The Kraton) Wahyuhadi noticed as he waited to be summoned for a personal audience with Sri Sultan Hamengkubuwono X. He was nervous as he prepared for his talk. What should be said to convince the sultan to support their project? How does one address such royalty?

The sultan of Yogyakarta is the unelected government offi-cial of the Special Region of Yogyakarta. This sultanate predates the nation of Indonesia, and its authority is written into the Indonesian constitution. This arrangement was made due to the pivotal role of the region and Sultan Hamengkubuwono IX in Indonesia's 1945–1949 revolution against Dutch rule.[8] Sri Sultan Hamengkubuwono X, the son of Sri Sultan Hamengkubuwono IX, is both the third governor of the Special Region of Yogya-karta and the tenth sultan.

Wahyuhadi could never have imagined that he would find himself at The Kraton waiting for a personal audience with the sultan. Not that long before, while meeting with WMPY partners, he had—half in jest—proposed that they should try to get the sultan's support for their project. Little did he know that another meeting attendee, UGM professor Haryana—a key WMPY project champion—knew Bayudono. And who was Bayudono? He was chairman of the Yogyakarta Research Board and a close confidante of the sultan. Mubarika said she had talked to him about the project.

A few weeks later, Bayudono reached out to Wahyuhadi to learn more about the request. At the end of their meeting,

Bayudono promised he would find the right time for Wahyu-hadi to meet with the sultan to explain the details of the project. When Wahyuhadi heard this, he felt "as happy as a little child."[9]

But that happiness from when the meeting was well in the future was replaced by nervousness as the time approached to meet with the sultan. Wahyuhadi wasn't a scientist, and he struggled with how he would explain both the complex science and the scientific merit of the project. He decided to focus instead on what he knew much better: friendship and humanitarian causes. He had met Julius Tahija—founder of the Tahija Foundation—earlier in his life and remembered the man fondly. He decided he would bring with him Julius's autobiographical book, *Horizon Beyond*, to discuss Tahija's humanitarian and ethical values.[10] He also knew that Julius had a family connection with the current sultan.

Professor Haryana and Bayudono had provided Wahyuhadi with this incredible opportunity to meet the sultan, and now it was his responsibility to get the sultan's support for the project. Without that support, many local community members would remain skeptical. The locals respected and revered the sultan. His imprimatur on the project would be invaluable. Wahyuhadi knew that a lot rested on his shoulders, and he also knew that he might have only one shot to convince the sultan that the project was worthy of support—after all, it is not every day that you get a personal meeting with the sultan to make your case about supporting a science project.

The door opened, and the sultan waited for him. Julius's book in hand, Wahyuhadi walked in to greet the sultan.

This meeting reinforced the notion that sound science and rational thinking are important, but that personal connections and shared values can matter just as much, if not more. Wahyu-hadi's decision to bring Julius's book was a wise one. The two men discussed the book at length as well as Julius's deep friendship with the sultan's father, Sri Sultan Hamengkubuwono IX, which had spanned decades. Both men had supported the Indonesian struggle for independence during the revolution, and both had shared interests in humanitarian causes and the importance of living life with integrity, honesty, and kindness. The sultan was interested in continuing his father's and Julius's legacy. He also saw the *Wolbachia* technology as promising research that could improve people's lives by eliminating dengue fever. And, importantly, it was an initiative that was aligned with *Hamemayu Hayuning Bawana*, a guiding Javanese philosophy espoused by the sultan, which emphasizes "balancing the universe to achieve spiritual and physical happiness and the safety of human beings and living things."[11]

The meeting with the sultan went better than Wahyuhadi ever could have expected. He described the meeting: "We talked about the humanitarian paths of Sri Sultan Hamengkubuwono IX and Pak Julius Tahija. Sri Sultan told me that we had to preserve those precious legacies—the humanitarian values, integrity, honesty, and kindness. . . . The personal bonds between the late Julius Tahija and Sri Sultan Hamengkubuwono IX had convinced his son, the present sultan of Yogyakarta, to demonstrate his support for the *Wolbachia* project. 'We have to follow our fathers' paths in the pursuit of goodness and humanity,' the sultan told me during the meeting."[12]

A month later the sultan became an additional signatory on the project's memorandum of understanding. Not only did he approve the MOU, he ordered that funding from the provincial government budget be provided for the project. And he went even further than anyone on the WMPY could have expected. On a visit to the WMPY mosquito laboratory, the sultan not only gave his blessing to the project, he also gave his blood when he "fed" the laboratory mosquitoes by letting them bite him so they could raise the next batch of *Wolbachia*-infected mosquitoes for the upcoming field studies.

Wahyuhadi and the WMPY team were ecstatic to receive the sultan's generous support and commitment, a huge boon for the project. With his support, a lot of figurative and literal doors would open for them. Many community members who participated in the study even began calling the mosquito larvae bucket they were responsible for safekeeping the "Sultan's bucket" and made sure the mosquito buckets (like those in figure 5.1) were treated with the utmost respect.[13]

The sultan's said,

> I have a kind of moral obligation to make this project succeed. Therefore, I have shown my moral and spiritual support to all researchers and staff of the project to genuinely demonstrate that I really do care about the work they were doing for humanity. By showing this example, I was hoping that my people also support this project and all its related activities. This is again a manifestation of the Javanese philosophy of "*Tut Wuri Handayani*" (meaning that a leader or a teacher should give his or her moral support and encouragement from behind the scenes).[14]

MULTI-STAKEHOLDER ENGAGEMENT

Gaining the support of one important stakeholder (or stakeholder group) can be challenging enough, but how about when you have to deal with many different stakeholder groups with potentially very different tendencies and interests? A diverse set of stakeholders could affect and be affected by the outcomes of the WMPY's studies, as dengue fever is a society-wide problem

FIGURE 5.1 A community volunteer carefully places a mosquito
larvae bucket in a household.

and the Wolbachia technology could have a positive society-wide impact. Influential stakeholders in Indonesia could also stymy the WMPY team's efforts. Practitioners and scholars across business, government, and academia have spent considerable time studying and analyzing how an organization or partnership can engage effectively with multiple stakeholder groups to accomplish its goals.

Many academic and practical insights have been made about how multi-stakeholder partnerships can accomplish effective multistakeholder engagement (MSE).[15] Planning, monitoring, ensuring transparency, and engaging with a diverse set of stakeholders early and often are common activities for effective MSEs. WMPY had a unit dedicated to stakeholder relationships and engagement strategies. Its stakeholders liaison officer, Victorious Munasdi, provided some insight into the unit's specific strategies for engaging with Indonesian government officials (and other stakeholders) to make strong connections and earn their trust.

In Indonesia, government officials are notorious for being late. The project's staff already applied the Tahija Foundation's codes of conduct—start on time, stay on track, and stop on time, or SOT. At first, people viewed it as strange. Usually, they would have to wait for hours before any official came to their meetings. Gradually, the local people understood that we would maintain our self-discipline. This also manifested the project's virtues. . . . At first, trying to get in touch with heads of government agencies is like trying to hold an eel by the tail, so difficult. They are almost unreachable. . . . My first strategy is to connect with his or her subordinates. When I am trying to develop a relationship with government officials, I always build connection with the entire staff of that office starting from receptionists, office boys, security guards, and secretaries, to heads of sections.[16]

Munasdi also spoke about the power of preparation and personal connections.

One day, I had to meet with the head of a government who was extremely busy and hard to get to see. His staff told me that he could not meet with me because he was being hospitalized for a certain health issue. Without thinking long, I rushed to the hospital to express my concerns. From then on, we had a very close connection, and it was easy to get his support and endorsement. That was the power of personal connection. But of course not all officials are willing to do that. It was just one of my strategies to win their hearts. Before meeting them, I usually googled them, learned their social media accounts just to understand what types of personalities they had, their hobbies, and their interests. By learning their background, it would be easy for me to start a conversation before arriving at the core subject of discussion.[17]

Multistakeholder engagement was essential for WMPY staff throughout the decade-long project. Staff engaged iteratively with government officials at many levels of government throughout the project's duration. A later chapter will detail the stakeholder engagement strategies that WMPY used to engage with various local community stakeholders to gain their trust and participation.

Although the sultan—a critically important local government stakeholder—had been very supportive of the WMPY project from the outset, other important government and academic stakeholders were not as positive in their initial assessment of the *Wolbachia* technology. As mentioned earlier, Soenarto and Haryana had experienced this resistance during phase I. Similarly, Utarini and other WMP team members experience this skepticism firsthand while attempting to secure approval for phase III research in Jakarta.

Though Utarini continued to be bombarded with questions from government officials and scientists in Jakarta, she refused to entertain the idea of starting from scratch with only Indonesian-based mosquitoes. She became more and more downhearted as the heated arguments and accusations continued unabated, but she was not ready to give up.

But then, hope arrived in the form of Dr. Bambang Setiadi, a deputy minister at the Ministry of Research and Technology and chairman of the National Research Board. Setiadi, well respected by experts and officials, spoke in favor of the project and its importance for Indonesia. He had found Utarini's and O'Neill's presentations to the group of experts inspiring as a scientist, a government official, and a father. As a scientist, he believed the project's technology and the science were coherent and rational. In his government official role, he thought the government should support innovative research and be grateful that the research would be privately funded by the Tahija Foundation. As a father, his son had suffered from dengue fever twice, a parent's worst nightmare. This project could have huge positive potential for Indonesia's scientific community to gain global recognition for cutting-edge science and improve the lives of millions of Indonesians who suffer from dengue fever.

Nationalistic sentiments should be set aside, Setiadi said, and this important research should be allowed to continue. He then suggested that an independent multidisciplinary risk assessment team of experts be formed that would monitor and audit WMPY for participant risk potential based on human subjects research best practices. If this team of experts deemed the risk unacceptable, they could recommend that the project be discontinued.[18] Ultimately, Setiadi's voice and idea helped save the day for Utarini, O'Neill, and the rest of the WMPY team.

In practice, this idea for an independent risk assessment team was put into effect as a chartered group called the Independent Data Monitoring Committee (IDMC). These independent experts were responsible for scrutinizing all safety aspects of the study and reporting their recommendations for study modifications or stoppage due to safety concerns to a newly chartered Trial Steering Committee (TSC). The TSC consisted of the study's principal investigator, two Monash University faculty members, and an independent Yogyakartan health expert. The TSC was responsible for supervising the project to ensure it followed established safety protocols and considered any new information that could jeopardize participant safety. If the IDMC reported recommended changes or stoppage to this committee, it was obligated to formally respond and inform any relevant committees (e.g., UGM's research ethics board).

It was now full steam ahead for WMPY's phase III—the most complex and ambitious phase of the project. The other two phases were challenging and important in their own right, but this third phase was an order of magnitude more difficult. The science was sound and had proven viable so far, but field studies are much more challenging than laboratory studies. And the phase III field studies weren't just any ordinary field studies— they promised to be some of the most large-scale and ambitious ever implemented, not only in Indonesia but also globally.

Now that the government and academic stakeholders they needed to convince were on board (some more enthusiastically than others), the project partners knew they faced one of their most unpredictable stakeholder groups: the local community.

6

THE COMMUNITY

I t was January 2014. WMPY's phase II had recently been greenlighted after the positive results of phase I. However, not everyone was eager to participate in the implementation of WMPY's phase II small-scale field study. Warsito Tantowijoyo did not have to look at the faces in the crowd to know they were angry; he only had to look at the weapons they carried—some even had swords! Many of the nearly two hundred villagers packed into the community meeting room were visibly agitated, and he feared for himself and his colleagues. This neighborhood in the Sleman Regency near Yogyakarta had been identified as an excellent location for the second phase small-scale, controlled release of *Wolbachia*-infected mosquitoes. If this pilot study succeeded, the team could move forward with the all-important third phase: the large-scale field study experiments that would be necessary to demonstrate that the *Wolbachia* technology was a viable tool to eliminate dengue in the entire region (and possibly the world).

Now Tantowijoyo and other WMPY staff had to try to convince the community that this novel and complex technique was safe and that its members should be among the first people to try it. No easy task. It also did not help those myths and misinformation about the *Wolbachia* technology and their research project that had been spreading on social media and through word of mouth. The staff wanted to inform the community members about the logic behind their research and simplify the innovative and complex science as much as possible. This goal would be quite a challenge to begin with, given a skeptical audience, but it would be even more difficult because Tantowijoyo and his team were still learning the new procedures from the WMP Global team as the local team worked to create best practices for application in Indonesia. Tantowijoyo wanted to be respectful to the crowd, so he started to explain the *Wolbachia* project in refined Javanese, the most widely spoken dialect in the region. However, as he began to speak, a villager rushed up to him and grabbed the microphone from his hands. The community meeting went downhill from there.

GETTING LOCAL: THE SPECIAL REGION OF YOGYAKARTA, INDONESIA

To better understand the local community and context where the WMPY project took place requires diving deeper into Indonesia and a region known as the Special Region of Yogyakarta, on the island of Java.

Today over 3.5 million people live in this region,[1] with about 75 percent of its population residing in an urban environment centered in the city of Yogyakarta.[2] Religion is an important element in many Indonesians' lives, and the region of Yogyakarta is no exception: around 90 percent of Indonesian and Yogya residents identify as Muslim.[3]

The region has a long and diverse history, with many of its villages, cultures, religions, and historical landmarks dating from a thousand-plus years ago. Nestled in a low-lying area with the warm Indian Ocean to its south, mountainous regions to its east and west, and Mount Merapi (an active volcano) to its north, the Special Region of Yogyakarta is embedded in a lush tropical environment that has seen its share of kingdoms and empires throughout the centuries.

Starting in the seventh century CE, the area fell within the Buddhist kingdom of Śailendras. Later, in the thirteenth century, the Hindu Majapahit empire began to rule the area. In the sixteenth century, Muslim kingdoms took control. It finally got its modern name, Yogyakarta, in 1755, when Mataram Sultanate leader Sultan Hamengkubuwono I moved his capital to the area to try to get away from the Dutch, who were meddling more and more in politics on Java. This move may have helped the sultan avoid the Dutch, but it didn't work with the British, who captured and exiled his successor about fifty years later. The Dutch took the area back a few years later and established colonial rule that lasted for over a century until a few years after World War II. Shortly after the war, Yogyakarta became a hotbed of resistance (sometimes violent) against Dutch colonial rule and for Indonesian independence; it was designated as the capital of the short-lived Republic of Indonesia, which extended for several years before Indonesia gained full independence from Dutch rule.[4] The staunch support for independence from Sultan Hamengkubuwono IX and Yogyakarta was rewarded when Yogyakarta was designated a special region, with provincial-level autonomy recognized by the newly formed national Indonesian government.

This history is reflected in the area's diverse, eclectic, and historic architecture. Ancient Buddhist and Hindu temples dot the landscape along with centuries-old to modern mosques, churches, and synagogues, all juxtaposed against modern shopping malls, high-rise apartments, and avant-garde office buildings. The sultan's royal palace sits near the center of Yogyakarta City and houses the current ruler, Hamengkubuwono X, whose ancestor gave Yogyakarta its name.

Looming over the region throughout history has been Mount Merapi. Not only is Merapi an active volcano, but it is also the most active volcano in Indonesia, with a millennia-long history of major eruptions and no sign of stopping. Significant recent eruptions occurred in 2006, 2010, 2013, 2014, 2018, and 2020 (continuing through 2023).[5] WMPY staff were affected by Merapi when it erupted during their field studies and they had to periodically monitor mosquito buckets that becames covered in volcanic ash.

Unfortunately, as if residents of Yogyakarta did not have enough to worry about with an active volcano at their doorstep, they also have to worry about dengue fever. Yogyakarta's warm and wet tropical environment is a haven for dengue-infected mosquito hosts. There is some seasonality to dengue outbreaks (higher incidence rates in January to March), but dengue is ultimately a serious year-round concern.[6] Yogyakarta was also internationally known by many scientists; several influential scientists and studies had already been conducted in Yogyakarta.

These factors, along with the Tahija Foundation's history and connections in Yogyakarta, made it a desirable place to try this ambitious experiment to eliminate dengue from the area. But a spider's web of challenges and hurdles loomed in the socioecological environment of Indonesia. The WMPY partnership had to strategically engage with multiple, powerful stakeholder groups throughout a multiyear, multiphase endeavor. The partners had reached out to both national and local government officials, but now they really had to focus their energy and resources on various community groups and individuals to gain trust and participation.

George Tahija noted, "Another reason we went to Yogya was that the sultan had control there, so there were fewer riots, no scandals, no political turmoil. The sultan is the head of government, basically forever, whether it is an elected position or not, because of his family's role in the revolution. People in Yogya loved and trusted the sultan's family. So we wanted to work there with them."[7]

Stakeholder Liaison manager Victorious Munsadi put it this way: "Yogyakarta and its people were unique. Fortunately, our staff fully understands the local people's way of life. We approach them by adopting the Javanese philosophy. We have been trying to be in their 'shoes' when explaining the project and its impacts on their lives. That was the most effective communication and community outreach strategy."[8]

To keep a finger on the pulse of stakeholder concerns and respond effectively, WMPY developed a number of tools and methods to both explain a complicated scientific idea to stakeholders and keep track of how to build support with key stakeholders and community members. When confronted with local community pushback on the project in its early stages, the WMPY team responded promptly and meaningfully to improve stakeholder engagement. One communication tool they developed was called the "stakeholder inquiry system" (SIS). It was meant to capture, triage, and monitor all the community's questions and concerns prior to the study's interventions. Similar to customer relationship management software frequently used by large businesses, this two-way communication solution enabled dedicated staff to capture questions or concerns from multiple communication sources (e.g., face-to-face meetings, phone texts, smartphone apps, emails), triage these issues and direct them to the most appropriate expert, and respond to every single inquiry (and there were hundreds) with substantive responses.

WMPY's Communication Engagement and Knowledge Management team was responsible for managing the SIS for much of the project's duration, but the SIS system was designed so that each inquiry received from community members and other stakeholders could be redirected quickly to specific expert(s) or other project team(s) across the organization who were best equipped to answer the question accurately. Once a response was prepared, it was delivered to the stakeholder in that person's preferred mode of communication (e.g., text, email, face-to-face meeting, smartphone app). The process was designed to be a flexible two-way communication system whereby stakeholders could send messages on a wide variety of topics. These topics included study participants' reports on the condition of their mosquito containers, community leaders' requests for face-to-face meetings with WMPY staff, and stakeholders' support for the *Wolbachia* technology or refusal to participate.

Many benefits resulted from developing and optimizing this stakeholder communication system. The technical infrastructure and accompanying standard operating procedures implemented by staff allowed for a responsive design that provided local community stakeholders with the information they sought in a timely manner. This system became a veritable knowledge transfer superhighway across key stakeholder groups and WMPY units. The SIS provided project leadership and management with invaluable real-time information so that they could identify emerging and common community stakeholder concerns, inspiring interdisciplinary knowledge exchanges and new protocols to address those issues. It also provided a new lens for researchers and scientists involved in community engagement through which they could appreciate how their scientific endeavor was impacting the community. This wasn't just a laboratory-based science experiment tucked away in a controlled and safe basement—many thousands of people were being affected in real time by their study. Being so closely and continuously involved with stakeholders through the SIS and face-to-face interactions helped many of the scientists appreciate the immediate relevance of their work.

This substantive stakeholder relationship management investment followed from the WMPY partnership's values of accountability and transparency when managing stakeholder relations. The SIS solution helped nurture that key ingredient—trust—within the local communities as members recognized that their concerns were being taken seriously by the WMPY partnership.[9]

To prove that the *Wolbachia* technology was a plausible public health solution that could scale up to whole cities, the WMPY team knew they had to conduct field studies in a large enough geographical area to convince public health officials, yet the area still had to be of a manageable size to ensure that they could follow scientifically rigorous methods (e.g., controlled experimental designs) for an extended period without limitless resources. In one of their studies alone, they would be conducting a randomized controlled experiment over a contiguous geographical cluster of twenty-six square kilometers in a high-density area with over three hundred thousand residents. To have a realistic chance of success conducting such large-scale field studies in the Yogyakarta region, the WMPY team knew they needed to strategically engage with multiple local community stakeholder groups in meaningful and sustainable ways. They needed robust community participation and allies, or their project had next to no chance of succeeding.

Throughout the WMPY project phases, the organizational structure adapted to accommodate changes to research and governance requirements, but there was always a core group of experts and teams responsible for overseeing stakeholder relationship management and community engagement strategies. Teams addressing community engagement and stakeholder engagement, along with specialists, were always available to address questions about these crucial activities. Bekti Andari, a WMPY stakeholder engagement team leader, discussed the importance of the team's "integrated vector control management strategy,"[10] which identified and aimed to bring together a diverse array of stakeholder groups that included local administrative officials, community leaders, religious leaders, women's groups, and other volunteer organizations. The characteristics of each stakeholder group was mapped, including its interests, influence, and capacities related to the project's objectives. Each group and its members were seen as important actors who could help or hinder the common goals of the project. And these goals rolled up to the main purpose of the project: to eliminate dengue fever. Bekti identified the biggest challenge as gaining the community's trust:

> For me, trust is the key. Sometimes, trust must be fought for. Once we gained people's trust, we could easily win their hearts to work hand in hand. I was beyond logical thinking. . . . My team had worked extremely hard to reach that level of trust. . . . It took us time and energy as well as emotional ups and downs when dealing with the locals. . . . Before we could try to win over their hearts, we had to be trustworthy persons ourselves. We had to show our genuine feeling, our passions when delivering the messages to make them more compelling and trustworthy. However, work had never been smooth. Many times, we failed to connect with the locals. Some of them fiercely rejected the project and closed the door to communication. We had to anticipate that such things could arise in the course of our work. What we needed was to mitigate any possible constraints and refusals from the affected community.[11]

To gain as much local community member participation and buy-in as possible, the project teams developed communication strategies to translate the complex scientific language associated with the study into messages that would be clearly understood and resonate with each group. Those messages had to be not only accurate but also attractive to residents. Before strategizing about how exactly to formulate and implement these messages, Andari and her colleagues went on community reconnaissance forays in the planned study areas to observe and better understand local customs and social structures. They made a point of studying how local community members made family and community-based decisions on issues related to their health and well-being.

After these stakeholder-focused information-gathering sessions, Andari and her team developed communication strategies that would be meaningful and sustainable for each identified target audience, as well as public participation metrics. Ultimately, their herculean task was an attempt to mainstream the counterintuitive and unusual method that the WMPY project needed to implement for its *Wolbachia*-technology solution so it could gain a critical mass of community support and participation. They knew this was going to be the opposite of easy. Consider it from a community member's perspective. You are being told that thousands upon thousands of bacteria-infected mosquitoes—infected with a bacterium that has a strange, foreign-sounding name, no less—would be released into your neighborhood and that this is important research that could be a really good thing for you, your family, and your community. In other words, you are being asked, "Please trust us."

Building trust was the key concern—trust between WMPY staff and community members was the social capital that needed to be invested in and accrued or the field studies would be nonstarters. To this end, Andari and her team put in long hours and considerable effort meeting with many diverse stakeholder groups and community members to gain and earn their trust. Andari's team saw all these stakeholders not as barriers but as bridges that could help her group make it to the other side (i.e., meet their project's goals). Their mindset was that it was important to respond to stakeholder concerns with constructive solutions and include them in the decision-making processes as much as possible.

Process transparency also helped assuage community concerns. For example, to determine which neighborhoods would receive the *Wolbachia*-infected mosquitoes and which would be the control neighborhoods (i.e., no *Wolbachia*-infected mosquitoes released) in one of WMPY's phase III studies, Andari suggested that the decision be made via a public lottery. The benefit of this approach was that it would alleviate possible concerns from community members that backdoor dealings or bribery might influence the neighborhood selection process. WMPY staff invited community leader representatives from each of the study area neighborhoods to attend the random lottery event. Each community leader selected a plastic ball, labeled "yes" or "no," from many that were concealed in a container. A "yes" meant that neighborhood would receive the *Wolbachia*-infected mosquitoes. With this solution, community leaders were able to participate in the lottery results and could see exactly how each neighborhood was selected in a random and fair process. Community leader representatives were also informed that as a thank you from the Tahija Foundation, and with the proper approvals, all neighborhoods would receive the *Wolbachia*-infected mosquitoes after the official study was over. No one challenged the random lottery results.

These inclusive and transparent stakeholder engagement strategies and activities did not make the WMPY staff's jobs any easier; their years-long journey was an emotional rollercoaster ride. While it is unlikely that Tantowijoyo and WMPY staff expected to have to face villagers brandishing weapons while engaging with community stakeholders—they knew they would face some resistance. The upfront stakeholder relationship management and communication preparatory work enabled them to create action plans to not just reduce refusal rates but get many community stakeholders actively participating throughout the duration of the project.

WMPY developed a stakeholder engagement approach that it labeled the "public acceptance model"—the same name given to a similar WMP community engagement model during the Australian field studies. This multichannel, multipronged stakeholder engagement model was based on the stakeholder engagement principles of the WMPY partnership, as well as lessons learned from the Tahija Foundation's previous Yogyakarta-based Sumilarv field studies and WMP Global's previous field studies in Australia.

Prior to the implementation of each field study in the designated study areas, a community engagement framework was employed that generally included the following activities.[12]

- Administering surveys to gauge community acceptance for releasing *Wolbachia*-infected mosquitoes.
- Engaging with existing community councils at the village level to create a "community reference group," with which WMPY could regularly communicate about the project.
- Coordinating with public health center (*Puskesmas*) staff to share project information with local residents.
- Attending existing community meetings and events to share project information.
- Setting up field offices in each location so local residents could meet WMPY staff in person.

- Managing an issues management system that enabled community members to contact WMPY via multiple methods (email, phone, etc.).
- Establishing a core group of "community champions" who were respected in the community and who could act as mediators between WMPY and residents when concerns arose. Local women's health collaborators (e.g., Family Welfare Movement volunteers) were always included in these groups, and the community champions also helped ensure that the project was aligned with extant government dengue control policies.

These were just some of the high-level engagement activities that WMPY employed to improve community acceptance and participation in the upcoming studies. And the foregoing list only scratches the surface of the extent to which engagement activities were tailored based on the local neighborhood, demographic groups, or even individual residents.

GOING HYPER-LOCAL

Given the nature of this field study, to achieve WMPY's goals, there was no getting around the fact that one of the most important and time-honored stakeholder engagement strategies was face-to-face and door-to-door interactions with community stakeholders. Prior to and during deployment, dozens of staff across numerous teams engaged in numerous face-to-face group meetings with local and regional community leaders and community group representatives. And they held a lot of group meetings. In preparation for phase II alone, almost three hundred community meetings were held with local community representatives to discuss the project and listen to their concerns. Hundreds more took place throughout all phases of the project.

Also, regardless of the type of engagement, the Tahija family and its foundation's values strongly influenced the WMPY team's culture and community stakeholder interactions. Humility, compassion, empathy, and integrity were values instilled in WMPY staff. Another key tenet adopted by the community and stakeholder engagement teams was that to be trusted, one needed to be trustworthy. As noted in an earlier chapter, staff were expected to follow the SOT method: "start on time, stay on track, and stop on time."[13] Greeting everyone with a smile, they were to be polite and personable in their interactions, whether meeting with a local villager to see if they would deploy a mosquito bucket in their home or a high-ranking ministry official to provide the latest updates on the project. Another method that put their values into practice was the "4S protocol":[14]

- *Salam* (Greetings)
- *Senyum* (Smile)
- *Sopan* (Pay respect)
- *Sehat* (Be healthy).

This values-based interaction schema was utilized by dozens of field staff, each of whom engaged with hundreds of residents during these studies. This value-oriented stakeholder relationship management strategy was surprising for some. For example, people were accustomed to having to wait hours for officials to show up at scheduled meetings, but this strategy built trust over time among the various stakeholders. It conveyed that WMPY staff took their jobs seriously, that they were from reputable institutions, and that they truly cared about the health and well-being of the stakeholders.

Tahija Foundation organizational values were put into practice as effective multistakeholder communication and relationship management strategies. They worked well, but that doesn't
mean no conflict or improvements occurred after stakeholder
interactions. As Tantowijoyo and his WMPY colleagues encountered at their community meeting, not all stakeholders supported
the project—especially in the early phases. The WMPY team
listened and learned from their stakeholder engagements. Rather
than ignore or subvert contentious views, they invested more
resources in an effort to effectively address community members'
concerns.

Each neighborhood in Yogyakarta City, Bantul Regency, and
Sleman Regency had its own character and interests. This meant
that the community and stakeholder engagement teams field
staff could not apply the same standard operating procedures in
all those areas and expect the same result. And neighborhood
differences mattered—a lot. For example, WMP secured communal informed consent at neighborhood units in some villages in the Bantul Regency. Some village chiefs preferred this
consent approach after hearing about early project-community
conflicts in certain Sleman Regency villages; the chiefs wanted
to preclude that kind of conflict among their residents by repre-
senting their people at the village level in providing consent for
the project. In these cases, each elected leader (village chief) of a
Rukun Tetangga—a formal Indonesian administrative unit that
typically includes forty to fifty households—would give consent
on behalf of their community unit (even though individuals in
that *Rukun Tenagga* still had the option to opt out of the study
when field staff visited).

The WMPY team respected the preferences of each neighborhood, even though that could take extra effort or mean not
conducting the study in specific areas where they encountered

significant resistance. Fortunately, negative perceptions about the project from the various communities were a minority viewpoint, especially after significant community engagement efforts tailored to each neighborhood in the study.

WMPY partners also listened to village chief recommendations, which often involved holding regular meetings with community leaders such as religious leaders, local community champions, and representatives from other important groups in each respective neighborhood so information could be shared and questions addressed. One community volunteer group that was especially important for the project was the Family Welfare Movement (*Pemberdayaan Kesejahteraan Keluarga*), whose hard work and dedication for this project will be highlighted later.

Besides community group meetings for meaningful dialogue with residents, the communications and media team, community engagement team, and field entomology team developed informational materials and marketing campaigns localized to each community. WMPY staff knew the materials had to be attractive, accurate, and understandable for various levels of education and age groups.

Staff and project stakeholders knew they needed to reach as much as the community as possible in a short time. Religion was important for many Indonesians, so they met with religious leaders and attended religious gatherings to share project information. Music and the arts were a mainstay in Indonesian society, so they attended theater and music performances and poetry readings to spread the word. They erected informational booths at cultural expositions and sporting events. They worked with teachers who wanted to explain the project and dengue control to their students (figure 6.1). Indonesians often have large weddings, and some WMPY staff even attended these events to talk about the project. Video competitions were held for high school

FIGURE 6.1 Teachers dress up in mosquito costumes to help educate community members about the *Wolbachia* project.

and university students, who created media describing the *Wolbachia* project from their own perspectives.[15]

One of the most difficult issues throughout the project was educating stakeholders about a complex scientific process that often made no sense to the people of the community. They knew that dengue was caused by mosquitos, so they wondered, "How can releasing a lot more mosquitos help prevent dengue?" Andari recalled, "The biggest challenge for us, for me especially when leading the community engagement (CE) team, was to accurately translate the research project into clear and simple language and to precisely formulate public messages in order to provide the community with adequate understanding on the importance of the research and to amplify the benefits of the project to the people of Yogyakarta and affected areas. The tasks were immensely difficult, as the team needed to mainstream this unusual method of eliminating dengue by spreading *Wolbachia*-injected *Aedes aegypti* to their villages."[16]

Dense, text-heavy, complicated scientific terms would not be effective in helping local residents understand what the project was all about. For example, since *Wolbachia* bacteria was strange, foreign-sounding, and difficult to pronounce, the team localized and shortened it to "Wolly" so it was easier to pronounce in brochures, murals, children's coloring books, and adverts. Also, most materials shared with locals focused on pictorial descriptions of how the project would work and what the team hoped to gain from it. Community team leader Equatory Probowo recounted, "We created murals [figure 6.2]. A big canvas on the big walls with mosquito drawings would definitely get people's attention. With the murals, the community members were proud that they were involved in this game-changing project."[17]

These materials helped tremendously, but the details of the project's cutting-edge science involving injecting bacteria into

FIGURE 6.2 A local family passes by a large mosquito wall painting.

FIGURE 6.3 WMPY leaders help a child use a microscope to better understand the *Wolbachia* bacteria.

mosquitoes and crossbreeding them in a laboratory is difficult to grasp for just about anyone regardless of their educational background. WMPY staff and leaders went into the communities to meet with people on their own turf to discuss the project and explain, as best they could, the complicated science involved (figure 6.3). Still, that was not enough for some, who had to see it to believe it.

GOING DOOR TO DOOR: DOES IT GET ANY MORE "LOCAL" THAN THAT?

Arguably the most hyperlocal method to communicate with someone is meeting them face to face at their home. And that is what it took for many WMPY staff to get their message across

FIGURE 6.4 WMPY staff meet face to face with community members to explain the project and answer questions.

(figure 6.4).[18] During the field studies' consent-gathering and deployment phases, the community engagement and field entomology (FE) team members had to work around the busy schedules of village elders and community members who had day jobs. CE team member often would have to start work before dawn to meet family members for mosquito bucket deployment because one of the residents had to leave for work at dawn. Then that same CE member would have to visit a different family member after dusk to try to get consent from other family members.

One WMPY FE staff member, Wasini, recalled the challenges of working unusual and grueling hours under tight deadlines to collect individual consent from residents in communities in the Sleman and Bantul Regencies for the phase II study.[19] Within three months, her team of almost twenty community engagement and field entomology members were responsible

for gaining documentable informed consent for study participation from five thousand residents. Following research ethics
requirements, they had to make sure the information they shared
with prospective participants was clear and understandable so
the potential participants were properly informed about what
they would be agreeing to. These residents ranged from farmers, to truck drivers, to housewives, to elderly grandparents. Some
resided in opulent estates with house staff, and others lived in
small apartments with multiple generations.

WMPY rented a small house in the area, which served as
the base camp for its staff. Every single morning—they worked
seven days a week with no holidays for those three months—the
team met to coordinate and gather supplies before canvassing
the designated areas so they could obtain agreement from as
many study participants as possible to permit the placement of
mosquito containers. Maps and informational materials in hand
and *senyum* (smiles) on their faces, they set out to convince residents that releasing bucketsful of mosquito larvae infected with
a bacteria called *Wolbachia* in or near their homes was a good
idea. To say it wasn't easy is a gross understatement. Many were
skeptical, and sometimes field staff had to return to a household
several times and spend hours explaining the main objectives of
the project until the residents were satisfied.

FE frontline worker Wasini speaks to the challenges she
faced explaining the project's complex science and getting consent from participants:

> People kept saying that the mosquitoes were everywhere in their
> villages, why should they have *Wolbachia*-injected mosquitoes
> to add to their misery. Many times, we had to visit their houses
> several times only to explain again and again for hours until they
> understood our main objectives. It really tested our patience and

compassion because it was not their fault that they did not understand this complex subject. We had numerous attractive brochures written in simple language with colorful pictures and infographics to attract their attention and help clarify the process. One day, I had to visit a house with ten family members age over seventeen. This meant we had to obtain informed consent from the ten members of the family. Unfortunately, some of them worked in the morning, the others in the afternoon. So, I would wake up at four a.m. to prepare for my family's breakfast and then went directly to the house to catch up with those respondents before six a.m.[20]

WMPY staff worked diligently for months on end to garner project support in the local communities. The 4S protocol could be hard to maintain for WMPY staff, but this training helped them tremendously, as they experienced many novel and unexpected situations nearly every day. For instance, this protocol enabled male field staff to move on quickly after politely declining the invitations of dozens of young women in a red-light district of Yogyakarta—while smiling, of course. This protocol also helped when one staff member discovered that the door he had knocked to try to get consent belonged to the sultan's brother! He need not have worried, as the brother and his family treated him with kindness and even gave him generous gifts after the study.

WMPY staff on the ground in local Yogyakarta communities knew their hard work was building stronger community relationships and helping spread accurate information about the project. However, as many went door to door, attended community meetings, or watched local news programs, they also noticed how influential different media sources could be in shaping how local community stakeholders viewed the *Wolbachia* technique

FIGURE 2.1 Portraits of the Tahija business family (L-R): Sjakon, Shelly, Laurel, and George.

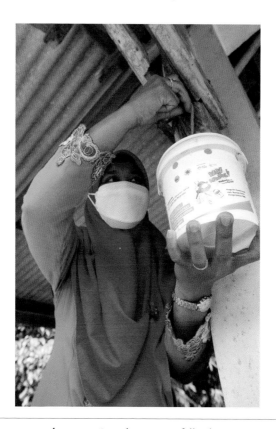

FIGURE 5.1 A community volunteer carefully places a mosquito larvae bucket in a household.

FIGURE 6.1 Teachers dress up in mosquito costumes to help educate community members about the *Wolbachia* project.

FIGURE 6.2 A local family passes by a large mosquito wall painting.

FIGURE 6.3 WMPY leaders help a child use a microscope to better understand the *Wolbachia* bacteria.

FIGURE 6.4 WMPY staff meet face to face with community members to explain the project and answer questions.

FIGURE 6.5 WMPY team members discuss information about the *Wolbachia* technology on a local radio show.

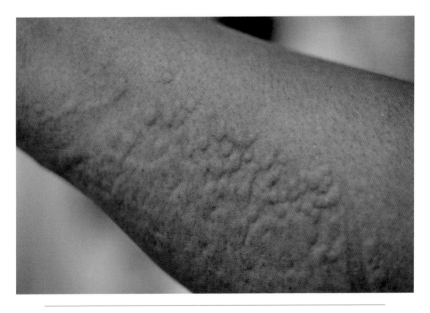

FIGURE 7.1 Swollen and itchy bites from female mosquitoes, a side effect of blood collection for breeding.

FIGURE 7.2 Members from a women's association known as the *Pemberdayaan Kesejahteraan Keluarga* (PKK, or Family Welfare Empowerment), a community stakeholder group involved in the project.

FIGURE 7.3 A WMPY staff member meets with community volunteers to discuss study developments and distribute materials.

FIGURE 7.4 A WMPY entomology team member works in the diagnostic laboratory.

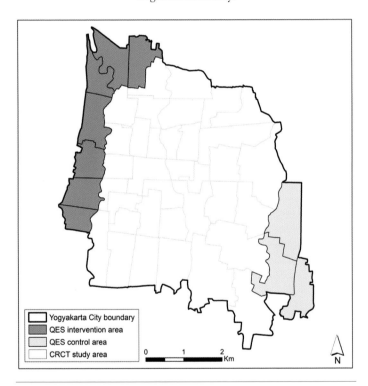

Yogyakarta City boundary
QES intervention area
QES control area
CRCT study area

0   1   2
Km

N

FIGURE 8.1 Map of the intervention and control areas in the Yogyakarta quasi-experimental study (QES).

Source: Indriani, C., Tantowijoyo, W., Rancès, E., Andari, B., Prabowo, E., Yusdi, D., Ansari, M. R., Wardana, D. S., Supriyati, E., Nurhayati, I., Ernesia, I., Setyawan, S., Fitriana, I., Arguni, E., Amelia, Y., Ahmad, R. A., Jewell, N. P., Dufault, S. M., Ryan, P. A., . . . & Utarini, A. (2020). Reduced dengue incidence following deployments of *Wolbachia*-infected *Aedes aegypti* in Yogyakarta, Indonesia: A quasi-experimental trial using controlled interrupted time series analysis. *Gates Open Research*, *4*(50). https://doi.org/10.12688/gatesopenres.13122.1.

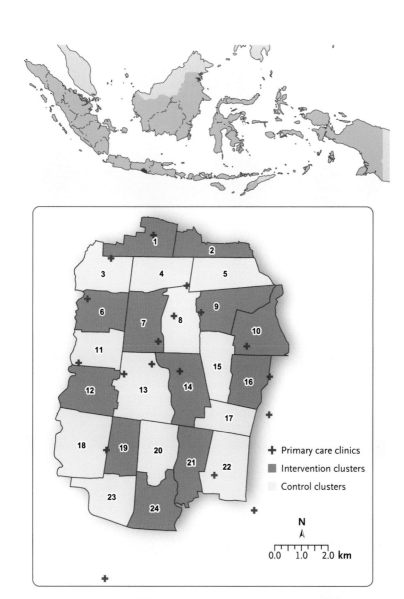

FIGURE 8.2 Map of the Applying Wolbachia to Eliminate Dengue (AWED) trial study site.

Source: Utarini, A., Indriani, C., Ahmad, R. A., Tantowijoyo, W., Arguni, E., Ansari, M. R., Supriyati, E., Wardana, D. S., Meitika, Y., Ernesia, I., Nurhayati, I., Prabowo, E., Andari, B., Green, B. R., Hodgson, L., Cutcher, Z., Rancès, E., Ryan, P. A., O'Neill, S. L., . . . Simmons, C. P. (2021). Efficacy of *Wolbachia*-infected mosquito deployments for the control of dengue. *New England Journal of Medicine, 384*(23), 2179. https://doi.org/10.1056/NEJMoa2030243.

FIGURE 8.3 WMPY scientists and UGM faculty gather in Yogyakarta.

FIGURE 9.1 Multistakeholder partnerships engaged in the *Wolbachia* project, including businesspeople, scientists, government officials, and community volunteers.

for controlling dengue. The advent of social media also makes it easier for individual community members to become media influencers. It became apparent that WMPY would need to engage these two intertwined stakeholder groups simultaneously.

COMMUNITY INFLUENCERS: LOCAL MEDIA, NATIONAL MEDIA, AND SOCIAL MEDIA

At times organizations can overlook the importance of the media as an influential stakeholder that can affect the success of a project. Social media can also quickly sway public sentiment in positive or negative directions. At first WMPY leaders thought it best to keep a low profile about their project on any form of media. Perhaps it was fear that the project easily might be misunderstood without the proper context or that it would be too distracting for their team. Regardless of the original rationale, the leaders quickly discovered that this strategy of keeping a low profile did not work.

Negative misinformation was also spreading on local social media channels about *Wolbachia* and the project's aims, vocal critics of the *Wolbachia* project were leveraging those outlets, including television and websites, to amplify their dislike of the project. The catalyst for abandoning the low-media-profile strategy occurred after a local Sleman resident effectively used the local media to oppose the project. The Sleman neighborhood rejection convinced CE team leaders that more resources needed to be devoted to media relations and media content whether they liked it or not. Their media and communications team spearheaded the media stakeholder relations and management effort. The team started slowly by distributing press

FIGURE 6.5 WMPY team members discuss information about the *Wolbachia* technology on a local radio show.

releases and holding press conferences. They first focused on building relationships with local media (figure 6.5), utilizing print and TV media, before eventually building up to national coverage. Articles were published in prominent newspapers, such as *The Jakarta Post*, *Kompas*, and *Bisnis*.

Once media relations became a priority, the publicity flowed. From 2016 to 2017, WMPY printed or broadcast nearly eight hundred pieces regarding the project. One staff member was also dedicated to monitoring all forms of media—social and conventional—so the team could quickly respond to any misinformation or disinformation. It became a balancing act of trying to avoid oversaturating the local market with project information while accurately informing the public about the project. Too much media exposure could backfire, but not enough could mean they might lose a critical mass of community support to negative publicity.

So, what impact did all these community and media engagement efforts have on community participation and sentiment? Did they matter at all for public acceptance? Rejection from some residents did occur—which was heartbreaking for WMPY team members after they had put in so much effort with each household. However, in the end their tireless efforts had a significant impact. For instance, after three months of seven-day workweeks for the phase II field study, Wasini and her coworkers ended up with consent from 95 percent of the targeted five thousand residents to participate in the study. Besides very high rates of participation across the phases, another quantitative measure of the impact of all these community engagement efforts was a pair of surveys sent to local residents prior to the study to gauge their acceptance of the release of *Wolbachia*-infected mosquitoes for controlling dengue.

For one of WMPY's large-scale phase III field studies, one survey was sent prior to the community engagement efforts and another survey after these efforts but before implementation of the field study. In the earlier survey, 67 percent of respondents were supportive of the project's method and 14 percent were not (the remainder were neutral or "did not know"). The later survey saw support increase to 79 percent, with 9 percent not supportive.[21] The increase in support from respondents between the two surveys suggests that WMPY's engagement efforts had a positive impact on community acceptance.[22]

These metrics only touch on engagement efforts that occurred prior to deployment of *Wolbachia* mosquito containers. Once implementation began, WMPY staff collaborated with participating residents to set up and monitor mosquito buckets for several months. Overall, the 4S protocol and CE strategies were so effective that some field staff even found themselves invited to funerals and weddings of the locals whom they had befriended through their frequent interactions (typically every two weeks) over the duration of the study. There were many heart-warming stories of friendships forged with and among WMPY staff and community stakeholders, as well as a shared sense of accomplishment for being part of an endeavor that could be so beneficial not only for their families but for the greater community. This was a collective journey of continuing education and mutual trust-building among the WMPY staff and the local communities.

As these CE protocols and others were being developed, behind the scenes—as phase II transitioned to phase III—the Tahija Foundation leadership began ramping up resources to start systematically capturing and cataloguing the knowledge gained from the community engagement and scientific activities. Gathering important information about tasks and processes would be beneficial for training new staff and developing standard operating procedures (SOPs), but in addition, what if this large-scale implementation of *Wolbachia* technology in Yogyakarta was successful and others wanted to replicate it in other areas? A roadmap for those efforts would be invaluable.

Staff were hired, and eventually these knowledge-gathering efforts would turn into the knowledge management (KM) unit, led by Ranggoaini Jahya.[23] KM staff needed to consider a broad range of questions when deciding what knowledge could and should be gathered. What critical information must be retained so that others could replicate the work? Which team members are the definitive sources for this information? How does one turn this information into an accessible and understandable knowledge base? What's the best way to capture this knowledge for posterity—video, audio, text? Is there information that should not be collected due to its sensitive nature?

Knowledge management was first housed within the CE team. Interviewing colleagues and shadowing staff, KM staff began to catalog what had been done in earlier phases and what was happening during Phase 3. At first, KM staff focused on capturing CE team activities, such as the community engagement programs, mosquito bucket release procedures, and safety guidelines. Since many CE activities were a multiteam effort, KM staff also branched out to gather information from the field entomology team, but they met resistance from some staff. FE team leaders Dr. Tantowijoyo and Andari did not always agree on community engagement practices and strategies. These internal historical tensions between WMPY team leaders in the CE and FE teams may have increased resistance to sharing knowledge with KM staff, especially in the entomology unit. Over time, internal resistance to knowledge management inquiries ebbed after staff transitions in the CE team, and the KM team was reorganized to be its own independent unit in the WMPY organization.

While internal resistance to sharing knowledge with the KM team waned over time, difficulties remained regarding how to coordinate with WMP Global's knowledge management interests and practices. By the time of WMPY's phase III, the global organization had become active in several other locations (e.g., Vietnam) and it had its own multicountry learning platform that WMP members could access and add content to for sharing what they had learned.

WMPY had been contributing to the platform to help WMP Global document and share SOPs based on what they were learning in Yogyakarta. But it was not always clear what WMPY should continue to contribute or expect to gain from this multicountry platform as phase III continued.

KM staff met with their WMP Global counterparts to try to get clarification about KM-sharing expectations and synchronize efforts, but problems remained. Many of the community engagement SOPs being implemented in other WMP Global locations were based on what was learned in Yogyakarta, one of the longest-running WMP locations. As one of the most advanced locations, what would WMPY gain from utilizing WMP Global's learning platform? WMPY staff use of the learning platform was low. Some of them were hesitant to ask questions about the platform when they did not fully understand something, fearing that they would sound foolish. Language translation issues did not help matters, as everything was translated into English.

But another overarching issue concerned how much procedures and practices could or should be customized for local community contexts (e.g., culture, customs, language, government) versus standardized across geographical locations. For instance, when the implementation of a small-scale *Wolbachia* field study in Brazil goes well, would those same procedures work as well in an Indonesian context? Were all the critical aspects of those Brazilian procedures sufficiently captured and transferred to the learning platform, or was some critical tacit knowledge still remaining in Brazil? And would anything be lost or confused in translation?

These knowledge transfer concerns and customization versus standardization tensions are not unique to WMPY and WMP Global. In fact, they are common across organizations from any sector that operate beyond a single site and community. A company needs to decide how much it should customize its product to be successful in a new market. A nongovernmental organization needs to decide how much to adapt its outreach strategy when entering a new country.

WMPY's strategic partners, and any other organizations that are interested in implementing the *Wolbachia* technology in the future, will face similar decisions. The viability of the *Wolbachia* technology as a global solution to the dengue fever problem depends on the right balance between tailoring community engagement practices to local communities to garner a critical mass of support and learning about which best practices can be applied across diverse communities. Tantowijoyo and his colleagues were finding out first hand what happens when a local community was not feeling that their concerns about the project were being properly addressed.

Fortunately, Tantowijoyo and the WMPY team members present at the tenuous community meeting described at the start of this chapter were physically unscathed following one of their most memorable community engagement events. The villager who had grabbed the microphone from Tantowijoyo said they wished to reject the program, did not want their community to consent, and were submitting an official legal document to the University of Gadjah Mada and the research team to stop the project. That was a disheartening setback for the team; however, it turned out to be a blessing in disguise. This rejection, as well as other instances of community pushback early on during the project, helped the entire WMP organization fully appreciate the critical importance of implementing its integrated vector management plan and public acceptance model. Community and media stakeholder relations were emphasized even more, as mentioned earlier.

At this meeting and many others, women were not only present in large numbers but leading the way by managing project teams, developing stakeholder engagement strategies, developing cutting-edge science, resolving organizational conflicts, implementing field study procedures, and much more. Without these women's leadership, this scientific and public health breakthrough in Indonesia would not have happened.

7

COMMUNITY VOLUNTEERS

Women Lead the Way

D r. Eggi Arguni faced a daunting task at the beginning of phase I of the WMPY study. She was to present a proposal to the dean of UGM's Faculty of Medicine and Public Health to win the school's approval to build a state-of-the-art laboratory on campus. To realize the WMPY project's goals and ensure ethical and safety standards were met, the school would need to build a world-class laboratory and insectarium in Yogyakarta. This proposal would enable WMPY entomologists to replicate the advanced *Wolbachia* techniques that WMP Global was using at Monash University. It would be a world-class research facility, but at that time, the designs existed only on paper and in people's imaginations. She had her work cut out for her, especially as a relatively junior UGM staff member who had arrived at the university from Japan only the year before. At first she had accepted an appointment as a local hospital pediatrician, but early in her new role, she received a call from Sofia Mubarika Haryana, who at the time was deputy dean for research and development in the Faculty of Medicine and Public Health. Haryana informed Arguni that some Monash University scientists wanted to interview staff for a new project. She agreed to meet them.

That is how she came to know people from Monash University and the Tahija Foundation. While she had a PhD in molecular biology and immunology and had worked on tropical and infectious diseases in Japan and Indonesia, she had never heard of Scott O'Neill or *Wolbachia* before meeting him at that interview. But she did know about dengue and was interested in working on eliminating it. When offered the job after the interview, Arguni accepted.

She got to know Tahija Foundation management and staff when they invited her to their office. Then, in late 2011, she traveled with foundation staff to meet with O'Neill and his team at Monash University. There she learned a lot more about their *Wolbachia* technique for controlling dengue and what it would take to develop similar infrastructure to replicate their processes in Yogyakarta.

In Yogyakarta, Arguni was expected to handle the day-to-day operations and capacity building for the nascent WMPY project within UGM. However, as any junior staff member in any hierarchical organization knows, having champions in positions of seniority can help make things happen that otherwise would not. For instance, these senior colleagues can provide access to meetings with those at the top of the organization's hierarchy. O'Neill asked senior UGM faculty members Yatie Soenarto and Haryana for help, and, despite their travails described earlier in this book, they got on board with gusto. These two powerful and respected women on the UGM faculty helped guide and support Arguni so she could talk to the right people within the university's bureaucracy to make the road less bumpy. And there were some bumps. It seemed that some senior faculty weren't always interested in seeing her succeed. Some staff would even say when she entered a room, "Congratulations, now we have an OKB member!" OKB is commonly known as an acronym for *Orang*

Kaya Baru, which translates to "new rich person." The Tahija Foundation was well known for providing generous pay for its staff and contractors compared with standard state university pay.

Despite some skepticism and difficulty with various staff members, Soenarto's and Haryana's support provided Arguni with the opportunity to meet with the school's dean—the person with the power to make or break the project. Soenarto and Haryana introduced Arguni to the dean and let her present the proposal for a new UGM laboratory and insectarium. If he approved, they could start building the infrastructure they needed for the WMPY project. If he didn't approve . . . well, better to think not about what that would mean for the project.

WOMEN'S ROLES IN INDONESIAN SOCIETY AND FAMILY LIFE

The WMPY project relied heavily on women like Arguni to lead at every stage and at all levels of the project's organizational structure. This is unusual because Indonesian society, though it does differ from region to region, is considered patriarchal and conservative regarding women's role in society and leadership compared with current Western standards. Gender disparities in employment and leadership positions have been stark historically. According to data from the World Bank, in 2020, only 52.5 percent of working-age women (i.e., fifteen years old or older) were active in the workforce compared with 83 percent of working-age men. A decade later, these percentages had barely shifted. And the underrepresentation of women in leadership positions was even more distorted, with only 19 percent in middle or senior management positions.[1]

This power disparity is especially acute for many women in Indonesia, as society strongly values deference for organizational seniority and a respect for elders, which imbues those in senior positions of authority with significant power and influence. However, Indonesia is rapidly modernizing. Women now hold positions of power in some government ministries and, as we have seen, in universities as well. Although it is a relatively young democracy, Indonesia has already had a woman president.

These workforce disparities may be attributed, at least to a certain extent, to the traditional societal norms of early marriage for women and their expected roles in family life. The institution of marriage is important in Indonesian society and often "determines women's economic welfare, their social status and their kinship networks."[2] Traditionally, women are expected to marry and, once married, to be the primary family caregivers, maintaining the health and well-being of their family members. Men are expected to be the primary breadwinners for the family. Considering the strong pressures to get married and the fact that marriage remains the key to opening doors n Indonesian society, women tend to enter marriage at a young age and have children soon after.

In Indonesia, the nuclear family composed of a husband and wife is still the fundamental unit of society; the wife is expected to run the household but play a subordinate role to her husband, who is the head of the family, or the primary authority, based on most traditional interpretations of Muslim family law. While Indonesia is seen as having more liberal views on Muslim family laws compared with Middle Eastern countries, its legal environment, religious laws, and dominant societal expectations solidify these gender-based household role disparities and authority inequalities between women and men.[3]

Yet, Indonesian women are not restricted solely to their household domain. The share of women in the workforce has increased over several decades, and in their work, they are not isolated from men. For women, generating income is "considered acceptable and even desirable . . . as long as it does not interfere with their family duties."[4] And especially in Yogyakarta, women have recently created channels through which they can increase their agency and control via employment and volunteering outside the home. In 2017, the *Badan Kependudukan dan Keluarga Berencana Nasional* (National Population and Family Planning Board) and its partners conducted a national survey of men and women in an effort to understand various current population issues. The impetus was to provide valuable information for policy makers and researchers to support the agency's vision for "realizing balanced population growth and quality families."[5] The survey investigated many topics related to family and work life, including women's empowerment, educational attainment, and employment statistics. Compared with women nationally, Yogyakartan women had a higher median number of years of schooling (8.6 vs. 6.0); a higher proportion of women had completed at least some postsecondary education (18.6 percent vs. 10.3 percent); and they had higher employment rates (68 percent vs. 53 percent), working primarily in the sales, services, and industrial sectors.[6]

However, breaking from tradition and shattering glass ceilings usually invites controversy, and empowering women to take on new roles of authority and power invites a lot of it. Efforts to empower women at the highest levels of government and spiritual leadership in Yogyakarta has caused a stir in recent years. In 2018, the sultan of Yogyakarta courted controversy when he changed his own title to be gender neutral. In addition, he renamed his eldest daughter *Gusti Kanjeng Ratu Mangkubumi*, which translates to "The One Who Holds the Earth," another gender-neutral title. These actions and others by the sultan and his immediate family are seen by many as paving the way to establishing the sultan's eldest daughter as his heir. That would be a big disruption to gender-based traditions.

A woman as sultan of Yogyakarta would represent a break from the tradition, hundreds of years long, of assigning only male heirs, and this distinct possibility upset brothers and sisters of the sultan. "We are an Islamic royal family, and the title is for a man. What would we call her—the sultante? It's impossible," exclaimed Gusti Bendoro Pangeran Haryo Prabukusumo, a younger brother of the sultan. He has even threatened to evict members of the sultan's family once the current sultan has passed away and has accused the sultan's family of being "power-hungry and greedy." In contrast, a younger daughter of the sultan has remarked about her parents, "I am very lucky to have parents that never said that is not a woman's job." She has held a leadership position in the royal court that was once exclusively for men.[7] The prospect of a woman becoming the sultan of Yogyakarta has caused significant publicly expressed discord among royal siblings, and this controversy has erupted in a region of Indonesia where women have attained relatively better education and employment than women in other regions.

More progress on gender equality seems to be on the horizon, as the women's empowerment movement in Yogyakarta and elsewhere in Indonesia continues despite pushback. In the 2019 legislative elections, women's parliamentary representation reached its highest level since independence—though it was still less than 22 percent of elected seats.[8] Women continue to find new channels to express their opinions and engage in political and social activism and leadership roles, but plenty of gender disparities, based on long-standing traditions and societal expectations, persist in Indonesian society. For instance, while women are increasingly encouraged to seek employment outside the home (or at least are not discouraged from doing so), they experience a significant gender pay gap, earning much less than men on average, indicating that systemic gender inequalities still exist.[9] They do not have as many high-paying job opportunities, and other issues of gender inequality (e.g., gender-based workplace dress codes) remain.

Many Indonesian women continue to bear the brunt of immense societal pressure to serve as the primary caregiver for their household regardless of their many other responsibilities. Given these expectations, the effects of dengue fever most strongly affect women in Indonesian society. Additionally, research indicates that infants and pregnant women are more likely to experience severe dengue than others.[10] To compound these equity issues, women now often are the key contributor to economic activity in the house; therefore, if they themselves fall ill or are otherwise negatively affected by dengue fever, their ability to earn income and stay gainfully employed is also jeopardized. Women have navigated these dueling gender role expectations and pressures for generations.

WMPY project leaders were aware of these gender dynamics in Indonesia and attempted to create an environment and foster working relationships based on gender equality while respecting local Javanese culture. Women often held key leadership and management positions in the organization. Key project allies in public health and community organization positions were women. The project simply wouldn't have succeeded without their crucial contributions.

TAHIJA FAMILY AND FOUNDATION LEADERSHIP

In 2013, Shelley Tahija, chairman of the Supervisory Board, and Laurel Tahija, a Supervisory Board member, took on formal leadership roles at the Tahija Foundation. Even without these formal roles, the two women were significantly involved in foundation and Tahija family decisions that ultimately led to their strategic partnership with WMP Global and UGM. Laurel's background in finance and economics, with a master's degree in development economics and international development from Johns Hopkins University, informed the Tahija Foundation's venture philanthropy approach to funding social projects.

Shelley had participated in the first Sumilarv project, attending some of the meetings. But once that project was judged a failure at eliminating dengue fever, she became more interested in whichever project came next (which eventually became the WMPY project), especially after she went with Sjakon to Cairns, Australia, to observe the *Wolbachia* field studies there. When helping to decide whether the Tahija Foundation would enter into another strategic partnership to eliminate dengue fever, she met with Duane Gubler, O'Neill, and WMP staff in Indonesia and Australia. As she learned more about how the whole system related to the *Wolbachia* technique worked and visited the mosquito laboratories, she became even more interested. Her background in pathology and significant experience working in laboratories helped her appreciate the science behind the dengue elimination technique. And this interest didn't wane once the project got officially under way. Shelley visited the mosquito laboratories in Indonesia and followed the WMPY project's progress throughout its phases, excitement growing as positive study results kept emerging.

WMPY PROJECT LEADERSHIP AND ADVISERS

New WMPY hires were required to attend orientation workshops to understand the expectations around the Tahija Foundation's values and behavior. Among the values espoused by and expected from the organization was gender equality. As Endah Supriyati, WMPY's diagnostic laboratory coordinator, noted as a key takeaway from workshop training, "[Gender] equality is another important thing, which is highly regarded at the [WMP] project. No gender inequality here." And this training did not appear to be merely an organizational training obligation; during the project Supriyati also observed that "many women became team leaders, even Professor Uut [Professor Adi Utarini] is project leader at WMP. Most of the lab and field staff are also women. I am very proud working with these intelligent and talented leaders and colleagues."[11]

Besides Arguni, Soenarto, Haryana, Supriyati, and Utarini, many other women led WMPY units at different phases of the project. Nida Budiwati Pramuko led the field entomology team, Bekti Andari led the stakeholders engagement team, Dr. Citra Indriyani led the surveillance team, Ranggoaini Jahja led the knowledge management team, Indah Nurhayati was an entomology coordinator for the mosquito-rearing unit, Iva Fitriana was a lab identification coordinator—and those are just some of the women with leadership positions.

These women were developing and implementing novel scientific techniques, management practices, and stakeholder engagement strategies as the project progressed in Indonesia. Indriyani led a team composed mostly of women, many of them nurses or midwives by training, who were responsible for monitoring dengue fever cases in designated study areas. At the outset at least one staff member expressed concerns about working on a team of mainly women. That concern may have been due to negative stereotypes, but there was also a cultural consideration, which the unit members wanted to recognize and address early on. As noted earlier, Indonesian women are more likely than men to be expected to stay home to take care of a sick child or loved one. This gender-based disparity in caregiver expectations may increase the likelihood of staff absences when a team is primarily or exclusively women.

Early in the process, Indriyani's team developed mechanisms and set expectations for staff related to sick leave plans. They informed staff about these staff backup mechanisms to fill in for absences when (invariably) some staff members would need to take sick leave, and they reminded staff about the guidelines again when absences occurred. Management understood the tensions that many women felt as both primary caregivers and productive team members and aimed to foster an environment of mutual understanding and support. Utilizing the "family" metaphor to describe employee-supervisor relationship expectations, the surveillance team wanted to make sure there was frequent and responsive communication between management and staff. Some conflict and friction were expected and should be shared; the most important thing was "how to deal with it together." Otherwise, the concern was that without communication, the "family is destroyed."[12]

Nurhayati, a senior WMPY entomologist responsible for coordinating laboratory mosquito rearing in Indonesia, was herself trained by Dr. Petrina Johnson and other scientists at WMP Global. She was flown to Australia as part of the knowledge transfer and training process to build Indonesian skills and capacity for reproducing and developing the *Wolbachia* technology in Indonesia so that *Wolbachia*-infected mosquitoes raised there could be released in the Yogyakarta field studies. She learned what she could from WMP Global experts in their Australian setting. In Indonesia, she discovered that new techniques and procedures had to be developed because they lacked sophisticated facilities and resources such as were available at Monash University. For instance, the Australian laboratory where they were trained had equipment that automatically adjusted temperature and lighting and cleaned the mosquitoes during rearing phases.

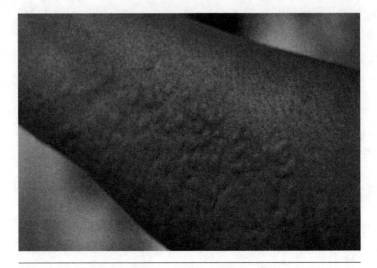

FIGURE 7.1 Swollen and itchy bites from female mosquitoes, a side effect of blood collection for breeding.

Lacking that technology, Nurhayati and her group had to manually clean thousands of mosquitoes, as if they were "bathing our babies."[13] This requires resourceful, determined, and dedicated team members. In addition, the female mosquitoes needed fresh blood to produce those "babies." Nurhayati and other volunteers allowed the female mosquitoes to feed on them and subsequently suffered the itchy, swollen side effects of numerous mosquito bites, which was above and beyond the call of duty (figure 7.1).

COMMUNITY PARTNERS AND VOLUNTEERS

Outside the WMPY organization and strategic partners, project staff needed the dedication and leadership of women and men in various local government, public health, and social organization volunteer roles to help them coordinate and implement WMPY field studies in the Yogyakarta region. Eliminating dengue fever would ameliorate a major source of sickness for the women who were the primary caregivers for their family members, a potentially huge upside if the study succeeded. But women would be also concerned about the possible health risks to their family when scientists planned to release many thousands of experimental mosquitoes in their neighborhoods.

During their work on the project, WMPY staff had the opportunity to interact with a wide variety of people across the social spectrum including lawmakers, religious leaders, and female market traders.[14] Staff members knew that women stakeholders in the local community would be the linchpin for their project. Staff collaborated with community health center physicians such as Ida Novirawati to monitor and track dengue fever cases in the study areas. Community health centers, or *puskemas*, are government-mandated health centers staffed with physicians, nurses, and other medical professionals to serve a broad range of local community health needs; they are often the first stop for any resident with a health concern. Prior to study implementation, WMPY staff consulted with these local health center staff to help in designing the field studies. They needed local medical professionals to help them monitor and track dengue fever cases and to know what was feasible for a scientifically rigorous approach in designated study areas. WMPY staff invited local medical professionals and health care providers to attend training sessions on the latest medical information about dengue fever, and health center staff were provided with diagnostic tools (i.e., NS1 antigen rapid diagnostic tests) that could quickly detect whether patients were infected with the dengue virus during the critical early stage of infection. During study implementation, community health center staff coordinated with WMPY staff to monitor and track trial participants.[15]

Women in government positions were also pivotal allies in supporting cross-sector coordination and communication for the project. Ryan Wulandari, in her role as a local Yogyakartan subdistrict government official, was responsible for coordinating and promoting health programs to improve her subdistrict's community health and well-being. The WMPY project fit within her portfolio of public health projects, and she provided the critical connections among WMPY staff, local institutions (e.g., community health centers) and local health volunteers (e.g., youth groups). Once the project communication content was finalized, she worked with WMPY staff to inform schoolchildren, neighborhood and community unit leaders (mostly men), and members from a women's association called the *Pemberdayaan Kesejahteraan Keluarga* (PKK, or Family Welfare Empowerment). She was motivated to create synergies and strong connections among community stakeholders to realize her dream of a community with improved living conditions, free of dengue fever.[16]

Of all the community stakeholder groups involved in the project, it would be hard to argue that there was a community organization more important than the PKK women's organization (figure 7.2). This volunteer organization, consisting primarily of women, has millions of active members nationwide and works on village development programs in well over sixty thousand villages throughout Indonesia.[17] The organization has changed names over the decades, but since the mid-twentieth century, it has been closely tied to various national government administrations. Starting in the 1970s, by ministerial decree, the PKK established connections at every level of administration, from neighborhood units to national levels of government through the Ministry of Home Affairs.[18]

FIGURE 7.2 Members from a women's association known as the *Pemberdayaan Kesejahteraan Keluarga* (PKK, or Family Welfare Empowerment), a community stakeholder group involved in the project.

PKK members are considered community advocates for societal and economic development, focusing their efforts at the village level. This organization is a powerful stakeholder when working on public health and social welfare initiatives in Indonesia. One local village chief went so far as to say that the PKK women were the "backbone of all social and health activities."[19]

During the COVID-19 pandemic, PKK was again a driving force in communities, promoting information about the virus and supporting vaccination campaigns. Driven by the principle of *gotong royong*, which translates as "mutual assistance," PKK sees communal work as a fundamental principle.[20] Unlike COVID-19, dengue fever has been a public health issue in Indonesia for decades, and the PKK volunteers have been responsible for informing their communities on and engaging in national health programs to prevent and eradicate dengue. These volunteers were already supporting the national government's dengue prevention and eradication efforts with other programs, including the 3M Plus, *Pemberantasan Sarang Nyamuk* (Mosquito Nest Elimination), *Satu Rumah Satu Jumantik* (One House One Larvae Controller), and *Ikanisasi* (i.e., distributing guppy fish to eat mosquito larvae) programs. These women went door to door, educating residents about dengue prevention and eradication practices and monitoring and inspecting locations to confirm good practices were being followed by residents in their area.

The Tahija Foundation and its previous partners had worked with PKK during the Sumilarv project and knew they would be needed again for the field study. These women were local community engagement experts; their knowledge of local culture and resident connections was invaluable for WMPY staff. Not only would the PKK's involvement provide legitimacy for the project and ensure it didn't interfere with existing dengue-related government programs, but PKK members were essential as study collaborators who assisted staff and participants in monitoring the study's mosquito larvae buckets and dengue infections.

Many women had been PKK members for years and even decades in their communities, building relationships and trust with local residents. And for a decade, women known as "PKK health cadres" were an instrumental mobilizing force to get community members to trust and participate in WMPY studies in the Yogyakarta area. They helped to socialize the *Wolbachia* method for dengue fever suppression with residents, many of whom were suspicious and skeptical about hosting buckets of mosquito larvae in their houses or neighborhoods. After all, these were the same species of mosquito that had infected their children—how could it be a good idea to release more of them? PKK volunteers were adept at helping WMPY staff present information in ways that locals could relate to and understand.[21]

PKK volunteer Ibu Eti's story is emblematic of the dedication and work of these volunteers. She recalled,

One day in early 2017, my son Evan, then a seventh grader, came home from school. He complained he got a severe headache with high fever. I was panicked and tried to measure his body temperature, which was a fever reaching forty degrees Celsius. I previously thought he was too tired after a soccer competition because his muscles were aching.

But he refused to eat anything and vomited any food that he tried to swallow. It was lucky he still wanted to drink water. After a few hours, it seemed that he could no longer stand his incredible pain, and we rushed him to the nearby hospital. He arrived at the hospital in a delicate condition and was immediately placed in the ICU ward. The doctor and nurses then undertook medical diagnoses and laboratory checks and found out that my son was infected with dengue.

The doctor told us that my son was lucky to be treated at the early stage before he experienced shock syndrome, which could lead to dangerous complications. Evan had to stay at the hospital and received intravenous fluid for five days to prevent dehydration. My husband and I were so grateful that he was able to recover slowly.

At the same time, there were seven other children in my neighborhood who also suffered from dengue. The children's parents were panicked and half angry with the staff of the *Wolbachia* project that had placed buckets in our houses and other places in my neighborhood.

These parents were suspicious that the larvae and baby mosquitoes in the buckets had grown into hazardous *Aedes aegypti* that had infected our children with dengue.

As a member of PKK who had attended numerous meeting and socialization of the *Wolbachia* project and how it worked to eliminate *Aedes aegypti*, I had a moral obligation to explain it to my neighbors, especially to parents of children who suffered from dengue.

My personal experience of having a child with dengue has allowed me to be more compassionate when dealing with parents with sick children. I felt we were emotionally connected with each other.[22]

PKK member Ibu Tari recalls how the process worked in most neighborhoods:[23]

Every RT, neighborhood unit, has assigned two PKK cadres to help FSO [Field Surveillance Office] staff, and I was happy to do that. Every day, I would visit houses in my neighborhood to find out about any sick children and adults. When I found one or two children with a high fever, I would immediately report it to the chief of the neighborhood, who would later pass it on to EDP [Eliminate Dengue Project] staff and local nurses and doctors.

When the sick child or adult experienced high fever for more than forty-eight hours, he or she would be taken to the hospital for further diagnosis and medical treatment. If the doctor found that he or she was infected by dengue, the neighborhood would conduct 3M Plus or eradication of mosquito breeding sites and clean up all the area within the radius of one hundred meters.

In addition to monitoring the buckets, visiting and reporting sick persons, PKK cadres and Field Surveillance Office staff held regular meetings every month. FSO staff provide us with necessary materials including posters to enhance our knowledge of dengue and other health issues, and especially regarding this research project.

To stay up to date on study information and coordinate their efforts, PKK volunteers attended monthly meetings with WMPY staff during the study periods to receive necessary materials (e.g., information posters) and learn about the latest developments that they could share with other PKK volunteers and community members (figure 7.3). These volunteers engaged in myriad activities to support the project and study participants in the community, such as visiting residents' homes to provide information (and help recruit study participants), monitoring study participants' mosquito buckets, and watching for evidence of high fevers in residents. Many PKK women were even "foster parents"

FIGURE 7.3 A WMPY staff member meets with community volunteers to discuss study developments and distribute materials.

for their own mosquito larvae buckets. They reported their field observations to WMPY staff on a regular basis. Coordinating with WMP field surveillance officers, the volunteers also helped identify and report instances dengue fever infection—at times even accompanying sick residents to their local community health center for immediate care.

These women cared deeply about the health and well-being of their community—and some might say they were the backbone of WMPY's community engagement activities. Of course, many men were also volunteers and leaders. The Tahijas and others insisted that "meritocracy drove the project." Success was achieved without racial or gender discrimination, and all the WMPY partners should be proud of that fact. Women and men leaders inspired thousands of volunteers to make the project work, from managing the buckets of larvae to keeping up with sick children. Stakeholder engagement and leadership was evident to the highest degree.

Arguni, Soenarto, and Haryana were persuasive in their meeting with the dean of UGM's Faculty of Medicine and Public Health, and he approved their mosquito laboratory proposal! They would be allowed to utilize two vacant rooms on campus to build the laboratory (figure 7.4). The Tahija Foundation agreed to pay for the advanced laboratory and its equipment, building this much-needed local capacity within UGM. Expert consultants were hired to design and construct the cutting-edge lab to meet the specifications required for their studies. When an expansion was needed for later project phases, the dean and other department leaders convinced the university's rector to repurpose a university-owned house to create an insectarium, where the entomology team had space for meeting rooms, storage, lab equipment and—last but not least—they could breed and raise millions of study mosquitoes. Renovating a house—which

FIGURE 7.4 A WMPY entomology team member works in the diagnostic laboratory.

would require a lot of tender loving care to restore anyway—into a state-of-the-art insectarium would be no small feat, but it also had to be done while preserving the historical house's exterior to retain the mandated architectural style of the university. Work on the building began carefully but purposefully, and it became operational as an insectarium for WMPY staff in 2013.

The entomology team was comfortable in laboratories (even with so many mosquitoes buzzing around), but many had to step out of their comfort zone to engage in community activities outside the lab to socialize the science behind the *Wolbachia* technique. This team would be part of a multidisciplinary community engagement team that also included experts in social science (e.g., anthropology, psychology, sociology) and public administration. Arguni often worked with Andari, who led the community engagement team in the project's first phase before leading the stakeholders engagement team in the second phase, and other WMPY staff to develop community engagement content and strategies. The CE team met formally and informally with all types of community groups and leaders to discuss the project and the science behind it. Their meetings took place at all times of the day, and even night, to respect the fact that local farmers and traders did not work typical office hours (e.g., 9:00 A.M. to 5:00 P.M.). Engaging with religious leaders and traditional village leaders was imperative, and the team also met with youth and women's groups. And it goes without saying that they met with PKK women.

It was not easy for the CE team to describe the complex science—that was still new to many of them—and the potential long-term benefits of the project to community members with varying levels of educational attainment. Additionally, they frequently need to present the information in the local Javanese dialect. CE team members leveraged many disciplines and perspectives to develop community engagement activities and strategies. Naturally, there was conflict as the team was composed of a mix of experts from the natural sciences, social sciences, public policy, and management. Expert opinions differed on what would be the best community engagement solutions.

But while conflict certainly arose (and not infrequently), several of those involved thought that not only were the solutions that emerged from this interdisciplinary approach better for it, their professional and personal growth improved from these experiences. And scientists who were used to working only in a controlled laboratory setting found their interactions with community members enriching. It helped them realize just how much the science they were doing would impact so many people in the world beyond the four walls of their laboratory . . . and insectarium.

The dedication, hard work, and leadership of the women highlighted in this chapter represent only a small proportion of all the women involved in the project who helped make it a success. And the fact that so many were in positions of leadership throughout all phases of the project and at so many levels is especially impressive given the backdrop of Indonesia's patriarchal society.

Arguni led the way as the study's principal investigator (PI) during WMPY's early years, helping build the necessary Indonesian capacity and infrastructure to conduct the project's successful phase I safety study in Yogyakarta. Then, she passed the PI baton into the very capable hands of another woman, Adi Utarini. Professor Uut led the complex dynamics involved in advancing cutting-edge science, multidisciplinary teams, and multistakeholder engagement to oversee the successful phase II small-scale feasibility study, demonstrating that the WMPY team should be able to implement the much-anticipated large-scale field studies for phase e—the crescendo of their project, which had been building for many years.

8

THE RESULTS

We have been implementing a large variety of methods to pre-
vent and eliminate dengue to no avail. I felt confident this
[Wolbachia technology] would become an effective solution
to reduce or hopefully to eliminate dengue for good. We needed
to try this technology in our city and surrounding areas. . . .
Every community group (Rukun Tentangga/Warga) has its
own characteristics, and therefore the WMP staff must also
adjust to this situation and apply a different approach in every
community. . . . With sweat, blood, and tears, the project team
members, along with local officials, have joined together to
work with the community right from the planning, trial, and
implementation stages of the project. It has always been a com-
bined effort of all the stakeholders.

—Heroe Poerwadi, Deputy Mayor of Yogyakarta[1]

IMPLEMENTING UNPRECEDENTLY LARGE
FIELD STUDIES IN INDONESIA

Prior to phase III implementation, additional experts from the
University of Indonesia (UI) and UGM were brought in to
discuss the complexities of the original study design proposed

by WMP Global and the best ways to measure the effectiveness of the *Wolbachia* technology over a large urban area. After much discussion, it was decided that the large-scale phase III study would be split into two distinct and complementary studies to test the *Wolbachia* technology's effectiveness in reducing dengue and severe dengue infection cases: a quasi-experimental (QET) design and a cluster randomized controlled (CRC) trial. The QET study had been proposed first by members of UGM and the WMPY team. While larger in scale than the previous phases' studies, it would be less complicated in design than the CRC trial that would follow; the latter's experimental design used methods developed for experimental clinical trials that are considered the gold standard for scientifically measuring effectiveness—in this case, the effectiveness of the *Wolbachia* technology as an intervention for reducing dengue infections.

The QET study would build from the previous phases' small-scale field studies and help the team build toward the more complex CRC trial, which became known as the "Applying Wolbachia to Eliminate Dengue (AWED) Study. This first phase III study would help the WMPY team gain additional experience deploying mosquito buckets, conducting community engagement activities, and collaborating with Indonesia's health system stakeholders to monitor dengue incidence in the designated study areas. It would help them refine large-scale implementation strategies and provide further evidence for whether the *Wolbachia* technology would be effective in a large and urban geographic area where dengue was endemic.

QUASI-EXPERIMENTAL TRIAL STUDY

The QET study was conducted in two geographic areas in the Yogyakarta region, one intervention area and one control area.

From August 2016 to March 2017, *Wolbachia*-infected mosquitoes were released every two weeks throughout the designated intervention area—a five-square-kilometers area with sixty-five thousand residents—with crucial help from about two thousand community volunteers. These volunteers, almost exclusively women from the neighborhoods in the study, coordinated closely with WMPY staff. The volunteers were responsible for protecting and monitoring the mosquito buckets that would impact their local communities.

Meanwhile, in the control area—at three square kilometers with thirty-four thousand residents—no *Wolbachia*-infected mosquitoes would be released. These two study areas were contiguous to, but did not overlap, the subsequent AWED study geographic area (see figure 8.1).[2] The two QET study areas were also not contiguous, separated as they were by the designated AWED study area.

Deployment and implementation went forward as planned. The prevalence of *Wolbachia*-infected mosquitoes in the *Ae. aegypti* mosquito population was tracked by trapping mosquitoes periodically for two years after *Wolbachia* deployment. In different subdistricts within the intervention area, the team found that the median *Wolbachia* infection rate among the *Ae. aegypti* population was 73 percent (ranging from 67 to 92 percent) after only one week of the final round of infected mosquito deployment, After two years, this rate rose to approximately 100 percent (ranging from 96 to 100 percent). In contrast, in the control area, they observed fewer than a dozen *Wolbachia*-infected mosquitoes over the same period.[3] These results indicated that the *Wolbachia* method, with significant local community participation in releasing mosquitoes, was extremely effective at spreading *Wolbachia* throughout the native *Ae. aegypti* population in the release area.

Besides confirming that *Wolbachia* was being successfully dispersing into the local mosquito population over the long

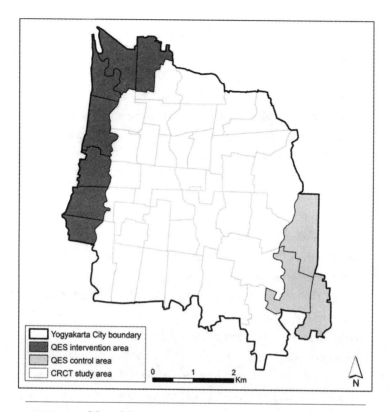

FIGURE 8.1 Map of the intervention and control areas in the Yogyakarta quasi-experimental study (QES).

Source: Indriani, C., Tantowijoyo, W., Rancès, E., Andari, B., Prabowo, E., Yusdi, D., Ansari, M. R., Wardana, D. S., Supriyati, E., Nurhayati, I., Ernesia, I., Setyawan, S., Fitriana, I., Arguni, E., Amelia, Y., Ahmad, R. A., Jewell, N. P., Dufault, S. M., Ryan, P. A., . . . & Utarini, A. (2020). Reduced dengue incidence following deployments of *Wolbachia*-infected *Aedes aegypti* in Yogyakarta, Indonesia: A quasi-experimental trial using controlled interrupted time series analysis. *Gates Open Research*, *4*(50). https://doi.org/10.12688/gatesopenres.13122.1.

term, WMPY staff collaborated with the Yogyakarta District Health Office and eighteen primary health clinics to gather and analyze monthly dengue fever incidence data from hospital records. With these longitudinal data (January 2006 through

March 2019) in the two study areas, they compared twelve years of monthly counts of clinically diagnosed dengue hemorrhagic fever (DHF) prior to and after the final *Wolbachia*-infected mosquitoes were deployed. When controlling for various factors not related to the *Wolbachia* intervention (baseline differences in DHF rates between the two study areas, seasonality, etc.), the staff's analysis determined that the *Wolbachia* intervention was associated with a 73 percent drop in DHF incidences.[4]

These were extremely positive results for the WMPY team and those living in the intervention area in Yogyakarta. However, given project timelines and the nature of this longitudinal research, WMPY stakeholders had no way of knowing just how favorable the QET study results would be at the time many of them began working diligently on the AWED study two years prior to the release of the findings. Also, there was little to no time for those staff producing *Wolbachia*-infected mosquitoes in the laboratory, nor those releasing them in the field, to reflect on their already considerable accomplishments. The final release of *Wolbachia*-infected mosquitoes in the QET study's intervention area occurred in March 2017, which was also when the AWED study's *Wolbachia*-infected mosquitoes were released in its randomly assigned intervention areas.

APPLYING WOLBACHIA TO ELIMINATE DENGUE (AWED) STUDY

For WMPY's stakeholders, the AWED study was the culminating large-scale field study that all the previous studies were building toward. It would be the most complex and challenging study they had yet undertaken. There was little room for error, and the utmost degree of scientific rigor had to be adhered to for the study design to withstand the intense scrutiny of the international scientific community and public health officials. The team had to follow well-established clinical trial practices without the luxury of a tightly controlled laboratory setting. The experimental setting would be daunting: an expansive area of twenty-six square kilometers in a contiguous urban environment of over three hundred thousand people. No small feat for any team of scientific experts.

The area was divided into twenty-four clusters approximately one square kilometer each. For the experimental design, the clusters were divided in half and randomly assigned as either an intervention or a control cluster. The twelve intervention clusters received releases of the *Wolbachia*-infected mosquitoes in between nine to fourteen rounds from March to December 2017, while no infected mosquitoes were released in the twelve control clusters. From January 2018 through March 2020, the WMPY staff collaborated with eighteen local government-run primary care clinics to recruit patients as study participants to track dengue fever incidence rates over the twenty-seven-month clinical surveillance period (see the AWED study map, figure 8.2).[5] Ultimately, more than six thousand participants were enrolled and met the inclusion requirements for the study. Over the course of the project, 168 million mosquito eggs were released into the area.

Study activities proceeded well for many months. WMPY staff were recruiting thousands of patients for the study, they were trapping mosquitoes that ultimately demonstrated that the estimated *Wolbachia* prevalence in the *Ae. aegypti* mosquito population reached a median of nearly 96 percent in the twelve intervention areas . . . but then tragedy struck before the study concluded: the COVID-19 global pandemic arrived in Indonesia in early 2020. It severely disrupted field operations and

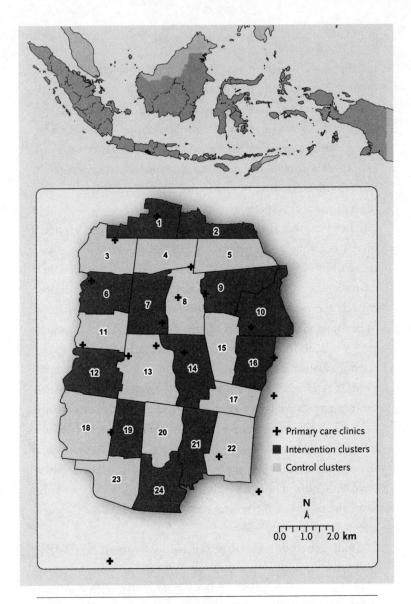

FIGURE 8.2 Map of the Applying Wolbachia to Eliminate Dengue (AWED) trial study site.

Source: Utarini, A., Indriani, C., Ahmad, R. A., Tantowijoyo, W., Arguni, E., Ansari, M. R., Supriyati, E., Wardana, D. S., Meitika, Y., Ernesia, I., Nurhayati, I., Prabowo, E., Andari, B., Green, B. R., Hodgson, L., Cutcher, Z., Rancès, E., Ryan, P. A., O'Neill, S. L., . . . Simmons, C. P. (2021). Efficacy of *Wolbachia*-infected mosquito deployments for the control of dengue. *New England Journal of Medicine, 384*(23), 2179. https://doi.org/10.1056/NEJMoa2030243.

required significant changes in protocols to keep staff and community members safe while attempting to finish the study.

Sadly, the devastating pandemic hit too close to home for some WMPY staff. In March 2020, Utarini's husband of thirty years, Dr. Iwan Dwiprahasto, died unexpectedly from the disease. A week later Utarini contracted the virus and was hospitalized for nineteen days. Lead scientist Dr. Riris Andono Ahmad led the project during Utarini's months-long absence while she stayed home with her daughter to mourn the passing of her husband.

Considering the serious safety concerns brought on by the pandemic, recruitment for additional participants ended on March 18, 2020. WMPY staff and volunteers continued their activities as best they could for several months until the steering committee elected to officially end the study on May 5, 2020. Fortunately for their study purposes, they had enrolled very close to the desired number of participants who had laboratory-confirmed "virologically confirmed dengue (VCD)" to detect whether their *Wolbachia* intervention had a statistically significant effect on reducing symptomatic dengue case counts. Based on their previous statistical power calculations, the team had wanted at least 400 VCD participants—they ended up with 385.[6]

THE AWED RESULTS

Even though they had not been able to recruit as many people with symptomatic dengue cases as their pre-analysis calculations recommended, the team ultimately had the statistical power to detect their *Wolbachia* intervention's influence on symptomatic, lab-identified dengue cases. The study results were not subtle.

In the study areas where the *Wolbachia*-infected mosquitoes were released, only 2.3 percent of 2,905 participants were identified as VCD compared with 9.4 percent of 3,401 participants in the control areas. These results indicated that the *Wolbachia* technology reduced symptomatic dengue cases in the intervention areas by 77 percent and hospitalization rates by 86 percent.[7]

The impact of these results spread quickly across project stakeholders. Powerful emotions were released—built up after many years of difficult work and the ever-present uncertainty about whether or not all their considerable efforts would be effective against dengue fever in the community. Tahija family members were especially affected. These study results, and the emotions the Tahija family felt when hearing the news, were the complete opposite of their previous project aimed at eliminating dengue fever from Yogyakarta communities. That one had ended in failure and much disappointment; this one brought success and much delight. Now, hearing the study results—77 percent reduction in dengue cases—and realizing the role they had played in the project's success gave the Tahija family great joy.

Shelley Tahija said, "Definitely an astonishing delight! Such a wonderful gladness!"[8] Sjakon Tahija claimed, "We were delighted. . . . Our family had played a key role in finding a practical, long-term, and highly effective way to prevent dengue epidemics. It is mind blowing that our family played such a crucial role in doing this. I hope after we are all gone our role will be remembered."[9] And George Tahija said, "I am very pleased for all the team members who had dedicated their time to this project. Very relieved for the family and foundation because we had spent so much time, money, and effort betting on this approach. The stronger emotional reaction I feel is seeing the empowered community members and how much this project meant to them. Of course, it is wonderful that the science has worked, but the benefits to the community in terms of improved organization skills and self-esteem is wonderful."[10]

Laurel Tahija:

> I felt uplifted and relieved that the team had successfully pioneered a new technology on a city-wide basis. I felt proud of each team member and their relentless perseverance to make an impact that could have national and global effects. . . . I felt grateful that the team had succeeded beyond a shadow of a doubt. I heard the voices of [Jean] and [Julius]. [Jean] declared this was "Wonderful" and [Julius], in his exclamatory voice, said, "*Luar biasa*" [extraordinary, outstanding] in my head. . . . It was a happy moment with I imagine lots of smiles on the Zoom screen behind the masks and in our foundation board room. I felt I was part of the family team in a way the four of us, second-generation Tahija family, hadn't all worked together before. It was a project that I felt would have made Jean and Julius proud.[11]

Tahija Foundation leadership expressed excitement and gratitude for all the government and community stakeholders involved (and were needed) to make the entire series of studies successful. Foundation CEO Trihadi Saptoadi expressed these sentiments well:

> As a venture philanthropy foundation, we are proud that our investment will surely bring sustainable impact. We are very excited and proud of this result. We [the foundation's board members] have discussed internally that the Tahija Foundation would like to finance the rollout of [the project in] Sleman and Bantul. . . . Support for the Sleman and Bantul deployment stages has

been the Tahija Foundation's and family's expression of appreciation to Sri Sultan Hamengkubowono X as sultan and governor
and the administration of the Yogyakarta Special Region. Not
only that, the Tahija Foundation and family is deeply grateful to
the people of Yogyakarta for their sincere and active participation
in making the project successful.[12]

The Tahija family members and Tahija Foundation were certainly not the only ones uplifted by the study results. The sultan
of Yogyakarta appreciated all that went into the WMPY project
and was hopeful about what these results meant for his community and beyond:

> We considered this one of the [Tahija] foundation's great contri-
> butions and efforts to help improve the lives of Yogyakarta people
> and the Indonesian citizens in the field of public health. Once
> again, I feel extremely grateful. . . . The *Wolbachia* research and
> implementation activities have provided new hope in our effort to
> eliminate dengue because it applied a new and different technol-
> ogy than previous ones that we had implemented. . . . I am hoping
> that the successes of these research and implementation activities
> can improve the lives of people not only in Yogyakarta but also in
> other places across Indonesia.[13]

Other government officials were also encouraged by the results.
Berty Murtiningsih, head of infectious disease control at the
Ministry of Health's Yogyakarta Provincial Health Office, was
involved in the WMPY project in different ways throughout
the years. Here are her thoughts after hearing about the results:
"Everybody in the government and local health community
consider this as good news, particularly for all parties working to
eliminate dengue disease, which has been haunting us for many

years. The results of the randomized clinical trial in Yogyakarta, which was able to reduce 77 percent of dengue cases in the city, have been so encouraging. It is so relieving that we have such a method."[14]

Many throughout the international scientific community were also excited by the astounding results. Those intimately involved in the study for many years expressed similar sentiments, as well as many other emotions (e.g., relief). They reflected on what being involved meant to them and expressed a sense that they did not have time to rest on their laurels, since there was so much more to do.

Dr. Riris Andono Ahmad, who had been working on the project since phase I, alluded to the euphoria associated with learning about the phase III results for those involved, "For us as scientists, researchers, that was a Eureka moment, the best time of any scientific work."[15]

Eggi Arguni, who had been so instrumental in developing WMPY's infrastructure in the early phases, mentioned how involvement in the project went beyond the scientific aspect for her: "I had never imagined [the project] would go this far, with national and international recognition. . . . It has enriched both my personal and professional life. . . . It makes me a better person."[16]

Warsito Tantowijoyo reflected on the importance of "shared passion," especially when working on a multidisciplinary team with lots of ups and down, and the impact of the project beyond its scientific import:

I am so proud of and thankful to my staff. Their passion and their dedication never faded in the last ten years. . . . Not all my field staff has an entomology background. One of them was a nurse, the others were from the social and communication sciences. . . . We have been through ebb and flow, good and bad times during the course of this project. There were conflicts among units, among individuals. But we are still standing strong because of our shared passion. . . . The *Wolbachia* is beyond scientific research. It is a noble work for humanity. It is science for humanity, and I am very fortunate to be able to contribute to this effort.[17]

WMP Global's Scott O'Neill was probably not alone in having mixed emotions after learning about the results—happiness and relief but also concern about future projects. "It makes me feel relieved . . . because I expected that the result would be good because of the work we have done. If the result was not good, I would be worried because we did not do it properly. I was actually relieved that the results came out so strong. I feel more than happy because it was so much effort." And from O'Neill's global vantage point, he also expressed worry as he considered the amount of future effort and evidence needed to make his *Wolbachia* technology a globally accepted solution. "I am just worried that even with the good results we have, I don't believe that by showing good results, something magically happens. And so, we need to make it broadly. . . . The evidence is all there, but people need to be more and more reassured that we can do it in three to five or more cities in Indonesia."[18]

In a similar vein, Utarini seemed pleased (and relieved) with the results but also felt there was little time to sit back and relish the results because the project team would lose important momentum for Indonesia's future:

These [results] were the work of our strong team. It tastes really, really sweet, but it just goes away swiftly. It was a relief to know the trial has been doing well so far. . . . I just cannot imagine the feeling of the Tahija family if the project fails after ten years of supporting and funding our research project. . . . The honeymoon period [of enjoying the good result] is over now, so let's think of what we are going to do next. If we stop this project, this will not be good for the country.[19]

Both O'Neill's and Utarini's future-oriented "the job is not done" perspective pointed to the reality of the original project plan. The end of phase III was never expected to be the end of the WMPY project if it went well. If the third phase was successful, WMPY was expected to transition its efforts to phase IV immediately: scaling up the implementation of the *Wolbachia* technology to expand within Yogyakarta region in a continued effort to demonstrate that it had the strong potential to be a viable and cost-effective global solution to dengue. And this implementation phase would require considerable adjustments in structures and mindsets. As O'Neill put it,

> We would really like to change this as a public health implementation as we go forward. Our focus will not be measuring anything precisely and generating high-quality evidence but how to implement it cost effectively, to be able to scale it up, to be able to cover the area more and more to protect people from dengue as quickly as possible. It is quite a change in how we go about implementing it. If we were to do the scale-up in Indonesia in the way we did in Yogyakarta studies, it will take three hundred years to cover all of these, and that is not acceptable for us.

THIS STORY CONTINUES TO BE WRITTEN

With the unequivocal success of the AWED study, phase IV was greenlighted in 2021. The fact that the *Wolbachia* technology was a scientific breakthrough as an effective dengue prevention solution in a densely populated real-world setting was now well known in Indonesia. The strategic partnership's main objective for WMPY's fourth phase was to prove that the *Wolbachia* technology could be a cost-effective solution to the dengue fever problem across a large geographic region. It was time to scale up the solution: more than three million *Wolbachia*-infected mosquito eggs produced per week, tens of thousands of mosquito release containers deployed, thousands of project staff and volunteers, and millions of residents in the area impacted.

The COVID-19 pandemic dramatically changed the original scale-up implementation plans, but the stakeholders found ways to do it safely. Staff and volunteer trainings were done via Zoom video meetings. Mosquito bucket deployment protocols needed to be redesigned to be aligned with COVID-19 safety guidelines. New strategies were developed to scale up implementation of mosquito bucket deployments in new communities in the greater Sleman, Bantul, and Yogyakarta regions in 2021 into 2022. As with each prior phase of the project, WMPY's organizational structure was redesigned, with some staff roles and responsibilities modified (and some staff let go) to align with a model optimized for large-scale mosquito production and *Wolbachia* technology implementation.

UGM and its faculty continue to lead phase IV efforts, along with their strategic partners. In addition, while developing ways to implement the *Wolbachia* technology in Indonesia, WMPY scientists and UGM faculty (figure 8.3) have developed new, patentable inventions, such a new type of ovicup (i.e., a device on which mosquitoes lay their eggs), a new mosquito bucket design that allows (study) mosquitoes to get out but keeps wild mosquitoes from getting in, and other innovations. Utarini was also recognized by *Time* magazine as one of its "100 Most Influential People of 2021" for her leadership on the project.[20]

FIGURE 8.3 WMPY scientists and UGM faculty gather in Yogyakarta.

The Tahija family and foundation are focusing on the phase IV implementation to prove that the *Wolbachia* technology can be a cost-effective and scalable globally. While eager to share all the knowledge they have gained from a decade of experience supporting the research and implementation of the *Wolbachia* technology, they have no plans to be directly involved in implementation beyond the greater Sleman, Bantul, and Yogyakarta areas. The hope is that other organizations across sectors will adopt and scale up this dengue prevention solution across Indonesia.

Within Indonesia there are promising signs that the national dengue prevention strategy includes the *Wolbachia* technology. In October 2021, the Indonesian Academy of Science (AIPI)— a government-sanctioned committee of leading Indonesian experts—delivered a formal letter to the Ministry of Health recommending that the *Wolbachia* technology be included as a ministry policy to reduce dengue hemorrhagic fever.[21] They cited the numerous favorable study results from the WMPY project, similar results by WMP Global in other countries, and an independent team's risk assessment that deemed the *Wolbachia* technology's public health risk negligible. This letter of recommendation by such a well-respected organization was an important step that may encourage government adoption of the *Wolbachia* technology in its portfolio of policies as it continues to develop its national dengue prevention and control strategy.

Even with WMPY's organizational restructuring to scale up implementation efforts, there is recognition that effective multistakeholder engagement activities would become even more critical for scale-up success: organizations with limited staff and resources simply cannot scale implementation across large geographical regions without strong partnerships and high-quality implementers in each local community. One of the biggest challenges facing the scalability of the *Wolbachia* technology is that a critical mass of local community participation is needed from each individual community. Dengue is a global problem, but existing solutions have always relied on localized interventions, and the *Wolbachia* dengue prevention method is no exception.

Deeply understanding the dynamics of important stakeholder groups in each local community will be critical for the successful adoption of the *Wolbachia* method. World Mosquito Program Global Regional director (Asia) Dr. Claudia Surjadjaja speaks to these considerations and the challenging road ahead for national implementation:

There are a number of determining factors that should be considered when applying research outcomes into implementation phases. Social, cultural, economic, political, and physical environments become our first considerations. We must also learn comprehensively about institutional settings including multiple stakeholders and demographic and epidemiological conditions. The infrastructure of the health system is equally crucial. This includes the roles played by governments, civil society groups, the private sector, and, more importantly, target communities. Applying *Wolbachia* technology's research outcomes into implementation stages and later to be included in Indonesia's national strategy for dengue prevention and control is tricky. Each stage has different challenges. Now, we have to shift the priority from research to implementation, in which we need to encourage community and local government to play key roles.[22]

It appears that effective multistakeholder engagement and trust building will be even more important for future efforts to scale the *Wolbachia* technology sustainably in Indonesia and beyond.

In addition to supporting WMPY activities in Indonesia, WMP Global continues to build from its experiences with those first field studies in Australia and Indonesia. It is conducting *Wolbachia* technology field studies in other areas of the world, including Bangladesh, Brazil, Sri Lanka, and Vietnam. Across all these studies, scientists have found dengue infections reduced between 40 and 98 percent due to the *Wolbachia* intervention method. There also appears to be a halo effect from this dengue prevention solution: preliminary results suggest that infections from other mosquito-borne diseases (e.g., chikungunya) were also significantly reduced.[23]

The consistently favorable results of WMP's *Wolbachia* technology studies across these countries prompted the World Health Organization's Vector Control Advisory Group, in late 2020, to recommend the WMP's *Wolbachia* technique as a valuable intervention against several vector-borne diseases.[24]

Another boon for the potential increase in adoption of WMP Global's *Wolbachia* technology was a 2020 study published by an international team of experts from Indonesia, the United Kingdom, and the United States. After analyzing intervention costs across multiple countries and estimating ten-year cost savings based on reducing costs to health systems society associated with dengue fever, they concluded, "*Wolbachia* releases in high-density urban areas are expected to be highly cost-effective and could potentially be the first cost-saving intervention for dengue. Sites with strong public health infrastructure, fiscal capacity, and community support should be prioritized."[25]

This study's cost-effectiveness results bode well for WMPY and WMP Global, given that its cost estimates did not consider WMPY's phase IV implementation, which is designed to reduce intervention costs per capita compared with previous studies. While these recent results in Indonesia and beyond are promising for scaling up this new dengue prevention solution, current efforts are still only a drop in the proverbial (mosquito) bucket: dengue fever infections continue to be a significant global public health problem, affecting hundreds of millions of people annually. The Tahija family and foundation continue to fund the deployment of the *Wolbachia* solution to the Sleman and Bantul regions (both adjacent to the city of Yogyakarta) but have no plans to expand farther. The *Wohlbachia* population has increased dramatically, as the project has released over 130 million *Wohlbachia* mosquito eggs. More than six thousand volunteers in community organizations have helped deploy the buckets.

O'Neill and WMP Global staff continue to apply for grants and talk with other philanthropic organizations in an effort to form other partnerships to research and implement their innovative dengue prevention method around the world. Meanwhile, the Indonesian minister of health, Budi Gunadi Sadikin, after analyzing the results and visiting the WMPY insectarium lab, has decided to adopt and scale up the project under the sponsorship of the Ministry of Health.[26] Eleven provincial and district governments are seeking to learn how to deploy the *Wohbachia* technology using an internship program called ACTIVATE. Areas for deployment include the cities of Bandung, Kupang, West Jakarta, Semarang, Bekasi, Center Lampung, and Bontang and the provinces of North Sumatra, Lampung, and Bali.

The Ministry of Health has given the green light to pilot projects using the *Wolbachia* method in cities with a high incidence or prevalence of dengue: Bandung, West Jakarta, Bontang, Kupang, and Semarang. It has formed a technical team in conjunction with four WMPY team leaders to serve on the ministry's *Wolbachia* Pilot Project team. Funding is drawn from the budgets of state, regional, and other legal sources.

9

LESSONS FOR THE FUTURE

This project's success was the result of many factors. Of course, good science, outstanding scientists, and technology are important parts of the story. However, it would be a mistake to attribute this remarkable success to these factors alone. As least four additional reasons are important to note as we distill the lessons learned from WMPY: (a) the role of business families in addressing societal problems; (b) the importance of establishing a purpose and values; (c) a remarkable stakeholder engagement capability that operates at a hyper-local level; and (d) an understanding of the role of multi-stakeholder partnerships. Each is crucial in understanding how businesses are changing the underlying narrative about what they do and make possible. Each is important for understanding business in the twenty-first century and the potential for business families like the Tahijas to make such a significant difference in their society.

THE ROLE OF BUSINESS FAMILIES IN ADDRESSING SOCIETAL PROBLEMS

Today, more than ever, we need to adopt a view of business as a partner in solving difficult societal problems. Sometimes businesses can invent technology to redefine and reframe the very nature of the issue. Sometimes they can be a key partner with governments and nongovernmental organizations, providing funding, expertise, and discipline. Individual businesses can take on some of the issues, but as the underlying narrative of business as more than just making money emerges, an even greater possibility exists when we consider the role of business families like the Tahijas.

In the dengue fever case, the Tahija family, through their foundation, provided funding and management expertise that enabled the *Wolbachia* technology to be further developed and deployed. Imagine the difficulty if the foundation had been excluded from participating simply because it was a part of a business.

Our underlying narrative about business in many parts of the world rests on the idea that business is fundamentally about responding to market forces with respect to products and services. In its worst form, this narrative says that "business is only about the money," and many believe that the only societal responsibility is to maximize profits for the shareholders or financiers. Unfortunately, this narrative also infects many business families, who do not see the possibility of making their societies better.

The Tahijas and several other Indonesian business families are innovative outliers of this "shareholder primacy" view. In the words of George Tahija, "It only makes sense to give back to Indonesia because in a developing society, our fates are so inextricably linked—when the people are doing well, we can do well. Also, in a developing society, government just cannot do this stuff. Literally cannot do it."[1]

And they are not alone. The last ten-plus years have witnessed a conceptual revolution in thinking about business. There is a renewed interest in businesses contributing to societal issues through ideas and organizations, including corporate social responsibility, sustainable development, shared values, conscious capitalism, "JUST capital," connected capitalism, ESG (environmental, social, and corporate governance) investing, and impact investing. The resulting new view of business, called "stakeholder capitalism" by many, has begun to be recognized as a better way to retain the benefits of a free-market economy while paying attention to all the effects of a business—both economic and social—on all stakeholders: customers, suppliers, employees, communities, shareholders, financiers, and so on. And this movement is especially relevant for business families that make up a large part of the private wealth in many companies in Asia.

The Tahijas also see an important symbiotic relationship between their for-profit and nonrofit enterprises. George Tahija explains, "I see the foundation and business serving our mission of elevating Indonesia in different and unique ways. Our 'reach' is greater having the [Tahija Foundation]. In a developing country where the government has limited means, nonprofits can play an important partnership role in achieving social good. The Tahija Foundation could not operate without funding and management experience from our for-profit activities. It's a symbiotic relationship that strengthens the presence, legacy, and reputation of the family in Indonesia."[2]

The Tahijas hope they have carved out a path that other business families in developing nations can emulate. While many business families are engaged in philanthropy, the Tahijas' philosophy of venture philanthropy enabled them to take on a grand challenge. By focusing on venture philanthropy, doing more than just writing a check in hopes of solving a problem, and by working together as a family, they believe that business families can have a significant positive impact on the development of a society.

THE IMPORTANCE OF ESTABLISHING
A PURPOSE AND VALUES

When the Tahija Foundation decided to tackle dengue fever in 2005, it did not do so lightly. The organization wanted to improve the lives of millions of Indonesians and, it hoped, millions more people around the world. The leadership knew that the task in front of them was not going to be easy. And they knew it would take years. It would have been easy for them to simply give up after the first project failed to achieve the results they wanted. However, because the decision to take on dengue fever came from an embedded set of values and purpose for the foundation and the family, they found a way to persevere that could lead to success.

Purpose and values are the most powerful leadership ideas that can be used to accomplish great deeds. First, they are aspirational as well as inspirational. Having a purpose and seeking to realize it gives meaning to our lives. Living with purpose inspires others to join in accomplishing it with us. When values are added to the mix—especially values such as honesty, respect, compassion, tolerance, generosity, and humility—many people can find within such organizations a place where they can live their best lives.

Purpose and values enable leaders to emerge at all levels of a project. Being clear about what you stand for encourages people to lead and act on those values with confidence that the organization is behind them. From foundation leaders to PKK cadres, many leaders emerged in the dengue project. And it was this idea of shared leadership that ultimately became one of the keys to success.

The scientific leader of the WMPY project, Adi Utarini, said, "For me, the *Wolbachia* project has more than a goal to eliminate dengue but more on healing the suffering of millions of people. . . . I thought my personal values were similar to those of the Tahija family. We all know they are very wealthy people, yet they are so humble. I have seen them directly interacting with people, how they respected their ideas and were willing to communicate with diverse people."[3]

Tahija Foundation CEO Trihadi Saptoadi put it simply: "I never thought that I would find a new project that would make me want to learn again."[4]

Talking about purpose and values is easy. It is much more difficult to use them to guide decisions. The Tahijas routinely conduct values training, and they reinforce the idea of their purpose in most everything they do. (Again, as noted in chapter 3, they learned this from the way that Julius Tahija led Caltex in very different circumstances.)

The WMPY scientist Endah Supriyati reinforced this view:

What really amazed me working with the Tahija Foundation family are the values that they have implemented right from the start. When I first joined in, there was a workshop on the values that all of the staff had to attend and strongly uphold. . . . We must respect others and the environment, have empathy, integrity, the must-have values for me, as a person, personally and socially, and we have to live by these values. . . . Equality is another important thing, which is highly regarded at the EDP project. No gender inequality here. Many women became team leaders. Even Prof. Uut [Professor Adi Utarini] is project leader at the EDP or WMP. And most of the lab and field staff are also women. I am very proud to be working with these intelligent and talented leaders and colleagues.[5]

There is no blueprint for which issues a business can take on, large or small, but it needs to be purpose driven and imbued with values that live in the organization. And there must be a commitment to making the stated purpose and values come alive in the organization. As Sonny Susanto, finance executive at the foundation, said,

> Yes, the values are not something just written on paper, but the commitments are very high, so we feel comfortable at work since there is clear guidance. We know there will be no strange things, since the values are implemented. Even if there is an obstacle, we discuss it together, so we remain straight, no bargaining. All is discussed, and solutions are found in line with these values. And this project for me is very interesting since I can see the family's extraordinary commitment. This is not an easy project. We could not see the end when we first started. We did not know whether or not it would be successful.[6]

Purpose and values are always connected (or should be) to the underlying systems and processes of an organization. Nowhere is this clearer than in the way the Tahija Foundation managed the complexities of the WMPY project. First, the leaders took an active role in project management, much more than merely writing checks to fund the project. George Tahija said, "we built a lot more controls into the funding mechanism, which was only given as needed, which helped the scientists shift their mindset. . . . The controls made the scientists feel like they had to meet targets before getting more funding. This worked better.

The Tahijas also knew that training workshops for new staff would be only so effective in prioritizing organizational values over time. To keep these values alive and well within the organization, value champions (VC) and value guardians (VG) were designated to help integrate these values into the employees' daily work. In this system, VCs were not necessarily senior staff; they were chosen based on how their behavior aligned with organizational values. Their responsibility was to facilitate discussions about the values that were being challenged and which solutions could be implemented to address those challenges. A monthly report from VCs was sent to organizational leaders (e.g., VGs, directors), who were responsible for taking action to resolve the issues and evaluating results. This system reaffirmed that living these organizational values was not just empty rhetoric. During the WMPY study, it was discovered that a nurse was falsifying records about the number of blood samples taken to test for the presence of the dengue virus. After the nurse was fired, the entire team was alerted to the fact that this person's actions violated organizational values.

These values, systems, processes, and metrics were strategically aligned. Laurel Tahija noted that while some of the metrics for the WMPY project were aspirational, the foundation had at least three kinds of metrics: "Well, we wanted to eliminate dengue, even if we didn't know our specific goals. We knew if we could eliminate dengue fever, we would start to see economic growth in the region. Also, we had goals around community engagement and goals around efficient and effective project management—like any business would have."[7]

After the Sumilarv project, the foundation knew that it had to take a larger role if WMPY was to be successful. Yet it also understood that its role was around project management and leadership and helping to eliminate barriers for the scientists and other team members. It continued to rely on its sense of purpose and values and to connect important issues like stakeholder engagement to the values.

A REMARKABLE STAKEHOLDER ENGAGEMENT CAPABILITY

As stakeholder capitalism becomes the norm in business, much can be learned about how to engage with stakeholders based on experiences from the WMPY project. First, fully acknowledging the importance of stakeholder support is crucial. As foundation CEO Saptoadi said, "Without the support of people in the community, we cannot create significant progress in this research, trials, and implementation."

Second, stakeholder engagement is a profoundly human activity. Of course, communication strategies and multiple efforts must be carefully planned and executed, but without a basic approach to treating stakeholders as ends in themselves, as worthy of attention, these strategies are likely to fail.

Community engagement team member Anastasia Maya Indah Lestari spoke on the necessity of treating stakeholders as human beings and on the intensity of the community engagement process:

> I was assigned to conduct a data-sensing procedure to get permission from local residents who were willing to allow the project team to place buckets containing larvae. At that time, I went to the Pringgokusuman subdistrict, the place I was familiar enough with. I spent many of my university years renting a house in this area. My close relationships with my neighbors during my school years in this neighborhood had widely expanded my chance to get as many respondents as possible in this area. It was a reconnecting and a renewal process of our previous close relation, *silaturahmi* in the Indonesian language. Do not underestimate kinship, friendship, and communication skills. They will become my opening

gates to implement the data-sensing process much easier and faster. This was the first step to implement the project, an opening door to the present project's accomplishment. . . . I usually start my conversation by asking about their families and short chats about the most trending topics in the local community. It is an effective easing process to arouse people's interest and curiosity about the project. I had to explain what *Wolbachia* is, how it works, and the impact on the people and their health benefits. In short, I have to explain things from A to Z to all the people I met in one office or institution. If they agreed to let us place the buckets in their places, it meant that I had to come to their premises every two weeks in a six-month period. I had intense interactions with people in those hotels, offices, and other places for six months. It was enough for us to be familiar with each other. The first impression was crucial in building trust. At Hotel Garuda, for instance, I have close relationships with parking attendants and security staff to the higher management staff. Some of parking attendants and security staff have become the foster fathers who took care of our buckets in the hotel areas. They also acted as educators to hotel guests who were curious about this project.[8]

Third, one of the biggest challenges in stakeholder engagement is to explain the project to stakeholders who may have very different points of view. Without presenting such clear explanations in an uncondescending way, trust simply cannot be built. Community engagement team leader Bekti Andari said,

The biggest challenge for us, for me especially when leading the community engagement team, was to accurately translate the research project into clear and simple language and to precisely formulate public messages in order to provide the community with adequate understanding on the importance of the research and to amplify the benefits of the project to the people of Yogyakarta and affected areas. For me, trust is the key. Sometimes, trust must be fought for. Once we gained people's trust, we could easily win their hearts to work hand in hand. I was beyond logical thinking. My team had worked extremely hard to reach to that level of trust. It took us time and energy as well as emotional ups and downs when dealing with the locals.[9]

UNDERSTANDING THE ROLE OF MULTISTAKEHOLDER PARTNERSHIPS

Finally, one of greatest lessons of the WMPY project is the potential power of multistakeholder partnerships (MSPs). WMPY has the potential to save millions of lives and much suffering, especially among young children. However, successful MSPs are complex. We can't assume they will be successful and effective just because every partner has good intentions. Many times, these partnerships involve organizations working outside their usual zones of operations, as partnerships may cross sectors. In this case, professors and staff from universities, businesspeople, foundation employees, scientists, government officials, and community volunteers all had to learn to work together (figure 9.1).

Andari spoke of the necessity for each partner to value the others and see their roles as interdependent: "The *Wolbachia* project has been a showcase in which all actors are intertwined. The Tahija Foundation as a philanthropic organization is dependent on the work of its partners, including the University of Gajah Mada, the University of Monash, Yogyakarta provincial and local governments, community-based organizations, and others to accomplish its goal. Interdependency is the key aspect for sustaining long-term partnerships.

FIGURE 9.1 Multistakeholder partnerships engaged in the *Wolbachia* project, including businesspeople, scientists, government officials, and community volunteers.

And Foundation CEO Saptoadi echoed this point:

The next thing I learned was about the form of this partnership. In the partnership there are Tahija, UGM, and Monash. How they work together must not be easy. Prof. Adi Utarini once told me it was the most essential element in this partnership—how to work together in harmony. I think herein lies the challenges, not just on how we work together to find the beneficial technology but also on a partnership in which all partners get the credit or good results. For me it is very important. . . . When we want to scale this up to other regions, we have to make sure that all partners are given credit fairly and justly, since there are philanthropists who provide funds but hope for nothing, only credibility and reputation.

Most MSPs are intensely local, and that is not very well understood by many partners. WMPY would not have worked without the engagement of all the partners at the local level in Yogya. The house-to-house process of gaining informed consent, working with the village leaders, enrolling the PKK and other citizens (mostly women) to work on the project, and even engaging local artists and musicians to play a role were all important. As WMP tries to scale up the results across Indonesia and the rest of the world, it is difficult to see how this could be done without a similar intensely local process.

George Tahija summarizes the challenge that WMP now faces:

> The new people are trying to take the project public, and to scale it with other partners. But it won't scale because community engagement has to be so high. There has to be local buy-in. And it has to come from the local people. Scaling is really hard because every town is "local" and most of the solutions are "global." But the mosquitoes are the sort of perfect solution. Mosquitoes are a local animal. People have local problems. Local leaders have power, and they can set up local barriers. The [Tahija] family kept the people from the federal government out of the way, prevented them from being a barrier, while we also worked with the local people. The family unlocked access to the local people and the local governments.

Since dengue first gained worldwide recognition as a public health threat, countries and experts have been trying to find an effective and sustainable solution to without achieving lasting success. The *Wolbachia* technology has the potential to be a global game changer as a complementary tool in the dengue prevention toolkit. The future of the fight against dengue is not certain, but one thing is certain: dengue fever is a society-level problem that requires a society-level solution. Many stakeholder groups collaborating across sectors are needed, and local community participation across diverse geographic settings is essential—not only for the *Wolbachia* technology, but for any complementary set of dengue prevention techniques that can be brought to bear. It is likely going to take much multistakeholder engagement, many multistakeholder partnerships, and multiple dengue prevention solutions to eradicate dengue effectively and sustainably across the globe.

As mentioned at the beginning of this book, this is a feel-good story: a story about long-term planning and dedication, ingenious innovations, and sustained collective efforts to tackle a societal problem, which culminated in an triumphant result—a long-awaited breakthrough that has the potential to turn the tide against a serious public health threat that has stymied public health experts for decades. Where this story goes from here will depend on which governments, organizations, communities, and individuals are interested in participating. The best part of this story about eradicating a global health threat may still be ahead. But it will take a global village of determined stakeholders to eliminate the scourge of dengue fever once and for all. Successfully eliminating dengue fever worldwide would be a truly feel-good final chapter to this remarkable story.

ACKNOWLEDGMENTS

We gratefully acknowledge the assistance of the following people during the preparation of this book: Tahija family members Sjakon, George, Laurel, Shelley; from the Tahija Foundation, Trihadi Saptoadi, Silvia Novi. Interviewer and translator, Rita Widiadana.

From the Institute for Business in Society, Joey Burton, Raphael Guimaraes, Nicole Fleskes, Megan Juelfs, Rebecca Little, Gaby Matheu, Jenny Mead, Eeshma Narula, Salem Zelalem.

We are grateful to Myles Thompson and the team at Columbia University Press for all of their support and hard work.

From the World Mosquito Program Yogyakarta, we thank Achmad Anam Tamrin, Adang Aristianto Kristianto, Adi Artanto, Adi Utarini, A Fadhilah Utami Ilma Rifai, Ardhina Ramania, Agus Subandiyo, Agus Susanto, Allan Alfin Nu'man, Anastasia Evi Handayaningsih, Anastasia Maya Indah Lestari, Anastasius Wahyuhadi, Anggarjito Sugiarto Estu Prabowo, Anggun Hatto Hanti, Anies Ariestanto, Anisa Parazulfa, Antonius Nur Kusno, Anwar Rovik, Ardli Swardana, Ari Rusdayati, Arief Rachman Hakim, Asri Nuraeni, Ayu Rahayu, Ayu Dita Larasati, Bambang Hardiko Nugroho, Bayu Satria Wiratama, Bekti Dwi Andari, Brigita Hevti Sukma, Budi Arianto, Budi Mulyono, Citra Indriani, Chandra Pradhitaningrum, Damiana Sapta

Candrasari, Dedik Helmy Yusdiana, Defriana Lutfi Chusnaifah, Desy Liana, Diajeng Kenanga Putri Ma'rifat, Dian Aruni Kumalawati, Dian Rosadi, Didit Sofiarto Munandar, Dwi Anggraeni, Dwi Satria Wardana, Dwy Desy Rahmawati, Dyah Wardani, Edwin Windyanto Daniwijaya, Eggi Arguni, Eka Nurul Azizah, Eka Rahayuningsih, Embun Majiid, Endah Supriati, Endang Pramesthiningsih, Equatori Prabowo, Erna Rofidah, Etry Novica, Eva Nusrima Yolanda, Evi Douren, Evy Gustiana, Fatika Ikhtariyani, Ferdy Azmal Fahrani, Finta Diarfarani, Fitri Ramadhan, Florentinus Dhanu Nugroho, Fradina Kiky Meilina, Gerardus Krisna Satya, Habibi Rohman Rosyad, Heri Wijaya, Heru Sulistyo, Hery Agung Susilo, Hilmy Ardiansyah, Ignatius Kleruk Mau, Imam Fungani, Inayati, Indah Nurhayati, Indira Diah Utami, Indriana Nur Hakimah, Inggrid Ernesia, Intan Prakasiwi, Irianti Kurniasari, Ismail Hidayat, Isnawati, Ita Ayundasari, Iva Fitriana, Iyxda Dwi Hartanto, Jatu Kartika Akmala, Juliana Purnama Putra M, Karnati, Katon Dwi Kurniawan, Kiswanto, Kiswiradat, Kunta Adi tetuko, Ktut Rentyasti Palupi, Laila Latifah, Lisna Hidayanti, Lyvia Iskandar, M. Ali Mahrus, Maria Bernadette Rindiyastami, Maryati, Merry Putri Wijayanti, Mifta Pratiwi Rachman, Mugiyanti Ikawati, Muh. Tamaji, Muhammad Ridwan Ansari, Muhammad Wisnu, Muhammad Rinul Fajari Wijaya, Munasdi Victorius, Murniawati Handayani, Nabhela Ayu Purwaningrum, Nandang Restu Sektiawan, Nandyan Wilasto, Nida Budiwati Pramuko, Nimas Suri Martiana, Noor Cholivah, Noravita, Novi Faturohmah, Novi Rustiana, Novita Hartati, Nunung Hidayati, Nur Faizah, Nur Khasanah, Nur Solikhah, Nurina Jihan Yulianti, Oktalia Nurfita Sari, Paulus Enggal Sulaksono, Pramidya Ujiana, Puji Rahayu, Puspita Zella Wigati, Putri Hardiyanti, Ragil Eva Agustin, Rahadyan Chandra Irawan, Rahmat Danu Wiranto, Rahmawati Ningrum, Ramadhan Kresnawan Hantarto, Ranggoaini Jahja, Ratna

Herlia Dewi, Resita Oktianty, Reza Yustian Dwiyani, Rifqi Zahroh Janatunaim, Rindhi Setyaningrum, Rini Dwi Utami, Rini Kurniati, Rio Hermantara, Riris Andono Ahmad, Risang Pandegan, Risky Oktriani, Rizki Sholeh, Roseta Irawati, Rudy Sigit Kurniawan, Sapto Wibowo, Sari Kurniati Pooroe, Sekar Langit Adesya Paramita, Seto Watugunung Rokhmatulloh, Shofia Eva Sagita, Sigit Setyawan, Siti Nuryanti, Siti Rochmatun, Soni Arianto, Sri Kurniati Pooroe, Sriono, Sri Yuliana Dewi, Sukma Tin Aprillya, Sularto, Sulis Mukaryanah Widarti, Supriyanto, Sylva Haryosaputro, Taufik Yuniar Wilaksito, Tilka Hujjatuna, Titayanto Pieter, Toto Selamat Mulyadi, Trihadi Saptoadi, Tri Kunarsih, Tri Mumpuni, Trismiyatun, Uswatun Khasanah, Uswatun Khasanah, Utari Saraswati, Viera Cristalia P, Vivi Leona Amelia, Vivin Fitriana, Wahyu Pranoto, Wahyuningsih, Warsito Tantowijoyo, Wasini, Wenny Widyastuti, Widi Nugroho, Winoto, Widi Nugroho, Wuriyatno, Yahya Mustangin, Yeti Meitika, Yodi Mahendradhata, Yuda Rasyadian, Yulita Endah Mayaningrum, Yusni Khafiyanti, Yusqi Taufiqur Rohman, Zahtamal.

From the World Mosquito Program, we would like to thank Andrew Turley, Ary Hoffmann, Ben Green, Cameron Simmons, Edwige Rances, Inaki Iturbe-Ormaetxe, Jack Brown-Kenyon, Jacqui Montgomery, Jessica Turley, Katie Anders, Peter Ryan, Petrina Johnson, Reynold Dias, Scott O'Neill, Stephanie Tanamas.

We would also like to thank our interviewees. From the Tahija family, Sjakon G. Tahija, George S. Tahija, Shelley L. Tahija, and Laurel C. Tahija. From the Yayasan Tahija, A Wahyuhadi, Trihadi Saptoadi, Sonny Susanto, Silvia Novi, Widi Nugroho, Michael Adrian. From WMPY, Prof. Scott O'Neill, DR. Peter Ryan, Prof. Adi Utarini, Riris Andono Ahmad, Warsito Tantowijoyo, Eggi Arguni, Citra Indriani & team, Equatori Prabowo, Bekti Andari, Indah Nurhayati, Iva Fitriana, Endah Supriyati, Achmad Tamrin, Ranggoaini Jahja.

Nida Budiwati Pramuko, Sigit Setyawan, Anastasia Maya Indah Lestari, Wasini. From the Scientific and Project Review Board, Prof. Dr. Ir. Damayanti Buchori, Prof Cameron Simmons, Dr. Tedjo Sasmono, Prof Dr dr Sri Rezeki S Hadinegoro Sp.A(K), Cameron Simmons, DR. Siswanto, MHP, DTM. From the Partners and Other Stakeholders, Prof. Ir. Panut Mulyono, M.Eng., D.Eng, Prof. dr. Ova Emilia, M.Med.Ed., PhD., SpOG(K), Prof. dr. Ali Ghufron Mukti M.Sc., Ph,D., Dr. Muhammad Dimyati, Sri Sultan Hamengkubuwono X, Drs. Heroe Poerwadi, MA, Ir Bayudono, MSc, Ibu Berti, Ibu Ari, Ibu Ryan Wulandari, Dr. Ir. Bambang Setiadi, MS, Prof. Sangkot Marzuki, Prof Yati, Seonarto, Prof Sofia Mubarika, Esther, Komunitas dan Kelompok Wanita Kelurahan Pakuncen, Komunitas dan Kelompok PKK Kel. Conkrodiningratan, Komunitas dan Kelompok Wanita Kali Code, Bp. Totok, Doctors & Nurses, Dr. Ika Septi, Nurses, volunteer, Dr Ida. From the Sumilarv Team (2004-2010), Titayanto Pieter, Munasdi V.

NOTES

INTRODUCTION: AN EXTRAORDINARY STORY

1. Yogyakarta should be pronounced as if the Ys are Js—as in "Jogjakarta," with a long "o" for the first vowel. Those familiar with this city often shorten it to Yogya (pronounced "Joh-ja").
2. Callaway, E. (2020, August 27). The mosquito strategy that could eliminate dengue. *Nature* News. https://doi.org/10.1038/d41586-020-02492-1.
3. The original name for the World Mosquito Program was the Eliminate Dengue Program, which changed in 2017. For the purposes of clarity and consistency in this book, we refer to it by its most recent name: World Mosquito Program (WMP). The Yogyakarta project, the main subject of this book, will be known as World Mosquito Program Yogyakarta (WMPY).

1. THE VIRUS AND THE MOSQUITOES

1. National Institute of Allergy and Infectious Diseases. (n.d.). *Dengue fever.* Retrieved January 9, 2024, from https://www.niaid.nih.gov/diseases -conditions/dengue-fever.
2. Prayitno, A., Taurel, A.-F., Nealon, J., Satari, H. I., Karyanti, M. R., Sekartini, R., Soedjatmiko, S., Gunardi, H., Medise, B. E., Sasmono, R. T., Simmerman, J. M., Bouckenooghe, A., & Hadinegoro, S. R. (2017). Dengue seroprevalence and force of primary infection in a representative population of urban dwelling Indonesian children. *PLOS Neglected*

Tropical Diseases, 11(6), e0005621. https://doi.org/10.1371/journal.pntd
.0005621 (correction at https://journals.plos.org/plosntds/article?id=10.1371
/journal.pntd.0006467).

3. World Health Organization. (2023, March 17). *Dengue and severe dengue.* https://www.who.int/news-room/fact-sheets/detail/dengue-and
-severe-dengue.

4. Selck, F. W., Adalja, A. A., & Boddie, C. R. (2014). An estimate of the
global health care and lost productivity costs of dengue. *Vector-Borne
and Zoonotic Diseases, 14*(11), 824–826. See also Shepard, D. S., Undurraga, E. A., Halasa, Y. A., & Stanaway, J. D. (2016). The global economic
burden of dengue: A systematic analysis. *The Lancet Infectious Diseases,
16*(8), 935–941.

5. World Health Organization. (n.d.). *Ten threats to global health in 2019.*
Retrieved January 9, 2024, from https://www.who.int/news-room
/spotlight/ten-threats-to-global-health-in-2019.

6. Centers for Disease Control and Prevention—National Center for
Emerging and Zoonotic Infectious Diseases (NCEZID), Division of
Vector-Borne Diseases (DVBD). (2019, May 3). *About dengue: What
you need to know.* Retrieved January 9, 2024, from https://www.cdc.gov
/dengue/about/index.html.

7. Doucleff, M. (2014, December 16). *Dengue fever strikes millions. Now
scientists hope to strike back.* NPR.org. https://www.npr.org/sections
/goatsandsoda/2014/12/16/370106655/hunt-for-dengue-vaccine-gets-closer.

8. World Health Organization. (2019, November 14). *WHO scales up
response to worldwide surge in dengue.* https://www.who.int/news-room
/feature-stories/detail/who-scales-up-response-to-worldwide-surge
-in-dengue.

9. Grant, H. (2019, December 1). Global heating driving spread of mosquito-
borne dengue fever. *The Guardian.* https://www.theguardian.com/global
-development-professionals-network/humanity-united-partner-zone/2019
/dec/01/global-heating-driving-spread-dengue-fever-asia-americas.
See also Karyanti, M. R., Uiterwaal, C. S. P. M., Kusriastuti, R., Hadinegoro, S. R., Rovers, M. M., Heesterbeek, H., Hoes, A. W., & Bruijning-
Verhagen, P. (2014). The changing incidence of dengue haemorrhagic
fever in Indonesia: A 45-year registry-based analysis. *BMC Infectious
Diseases, 14*(1), Article 412. https://doi.org/10.1186/1471-2334-14-412.

10. U.S. Food & Drug Administration. (2019, May 1). *First FDA-approved vaccine for the prevention of dengue disease in endemic regions* [Press release]. https://www.fda.gov/news-events/press-announcements/first -fda-approved-vaccine-prevention-dengue-disease-endemic-regions.

11. Rajapakse, S., Rodrigo, C., & Rajapakse, A. (2012). Treatment of dengue fever. *Infection and Drug Resistance, 5*, 103. https://doi.org/10.2147/IDR .S22613.

12. Gubler, D. J. (2006). Dengue/dengue haemorrhagic fever: History and current status. In Novartis Foundation, G. Bock, and J. Goode, Eds., *New treatment strategies for dengue and other flaviviral diseases: Novartis Foundation Symposium 277* (pp. 3–16, 16–22, 71–73, 251–253). Wiley. https://doi.org/10.1002/0470058005.ch2

13. McDermott, M. T. (2021, September 22). Even California has a mosquito problem. *The New York Times*. https://www.nytimes.com/2021/09/22/us /california-mosquitoes.html.

14. See World Health Organization (2023, March 17).

15. European Centre for Disease Prevention and Control. (2023, January 2). *Aedes aegypti—Factsheet for experts*. Retrieved February 12, 2024, from https://www.ecdc.europa.eu/en/disease-vectors/facts/mosquito -factsheets/aedes-aegypti.

16. See World Health Organization (2023, March 17).

17. Pouliot, S. H., Xiong, X., Harville, E., Paz-Soldan, V., Tomashek, K. M., Breart, G., & Buekens, P. (2010). Maternal dengue and pregnancy outcomes: A systematic review. *Obstetrical & Gynecological Survey, 65*(2), 107–118. https://doi.org/10.1097/OGX.0b013e3181cb8fbc.

18. Sánchez-González, L., Adams, L., and Paz-Bailey, G. (n.d.). Dengue— Travelers' health. In *2024 yellow book*. Centers for Disease Control and Prevention. Retrieved February 11, 2024, from https://wwwnc.cdc.gov /travel/yellowbook/2020/travel-related-infectious-diseases/dengue.

19. See Doucleff (2014).

20. Centers for Disease Control and Prevention. (2019, August 21). *Dengue— Clinical presentation*. https://www.cdc.gov/dengue/healthcare-providers /clinical-presentation.html.

21. Mayo Clinic. (2022, October 5). *Dengue fever—Symptoms and causes*. https://www.mayoclinic.org/diseases-conditions/dengue-fever /symptoms-causes/syc-20353078.

22. Alejandria, M. M. (2015). Dengue haemorrhagic fever or dengue shock syndrome in children. *BMJ Clinical Evidence, 2015*, 0917. https://www .ncbi.nlm.nih.gov/pmc/articles/PMC4392842/. See also Jamaiah, I., Rohela, M., Nissapatorn, V., Hiew, F. T., Mohammad Halizam, A., Noor Liani, H., & Siti Khairunnisaak, A. R. (2007). Retrospective study of dengue fever (DF) and dengue hemorrhagic fever (DHF) patients at University Malaya Medical Center, Kuala Lumpur, Malaysia in the year 2005. *The Southeast Asian Journal of Tropical Medicine and Public Health, 38*(Suppl.1), 224–230.

23. Centers for Disease Control and Prevention, National Center for Emerging and Zoonotic Infectious Diseases (NCEZID), Division of Vector-Borne Diseases (DVBD). (2020, January 24). *Dengue virus—Testing guidance.* https://www.cdc.gov/dengue/healthcare-providers/testing /testing-guidance.html.

24. Makroo, R. N., Raina, V., Kumar, P., & Kanth, R. K. (2007). Role of platelet transfusion in the management of dengue patients in a tertiary care hospital. *Asian Journal of Transfusion Science, 1*(1), 4–7. https://doi.org /10.4103/0973-6247.28065.

25. Schulte, A., Weber, I., Tiga-Loza, D. C., Larios, I. Y. A., Shepard, D. S., Tschampl, C. A., . . . & Ramos-Castañeda, J. (2020). Health-related quality of life after dengue fever, Morelos, Mexico, 2016–2017. *Emerging Infectious Diseases*, 26(4),751–755.https://doi.org/10.3201/eid2604.190729.

26. García, G., González, N., Pérez, A. B., Sierra, B., Aguirre, E., Rizo, D., . . . & Pacheco, B. (2011). Long-term persistence of clinical symptoms in dengue-infected persons and its association with immunological disorders. *International Journal of Infectious Diseases, 15*(1), e38–e43. https://doi.org/10.1016/j.ijid.2010.09.008.

27. Kusriastuti, R., & Sutomo, S. (2005, December). Evolution of dengue prevention and control programme in Indonesia. World Health Organization. *Dengue Bulletin, 29*, 1–7. https://apps.who.int/iris/handle /10665/164013.

28. Vong, S., Khieu, V., Glass, O., Ly, S., Duong, V., Huy, R., Ngan, C., Wichmann, O., Letson, G. W., Margolis, H. S., & Buchy, P. (2010). Dengue incidence in urban and rural Cambodia: Results from population-based active fever surveillance, 2006–2008. *PLOS Neglected Tropical Diseases, 4*(11), e903. https://doi.org/10.1371/journal.pntd.0000903.

29. Shepard, D. S., Undurraga, E. A., & Halasa, Y. A. (2013). Economic and disease burden of dengue in Southeast Asia. *PLoS Neglected Tropical Diseases, 7*(2), e2055. https://doi.org/10.1371/journal.pntd.0002055.

30. See Gubler (2006).

31. U.S. Central Intelligence Agency. (2024, February 6). East Asia/Southeast Asia: Indonesia. In *The World Factbook*. Central Intelligence Agency. https://www.cia.gov/the-world-factbook/countries/indonesia/. See also Leinbach, T. R., Wolters, O. W., McDivitt, J. F., Mohamad, G. S., Legge, J. D., & Adam, A. W. (2024, February 12). Indonesia. *Encyclopaedia Britannica*. https://www.britannica.com/place/Indonesia.

32. Lestari, S., King, A., Vincent, C., Karoly, D., & Protat, A. (2019). Seasonal dependence of rainfall extremes in and around Jakarta, Indonesia. *Weather and Climate Extremes, 24*, 100202. https://doi.org/10.1016/j.wace.2019.100202.

33. World Mosquito Program. (2023, June). *Indonesia—World Mosquito Program*. https://www.worldmosquitoprogram.org/en/global-progress/indonesia.

34. Huang, E. (2020, July 10). *Outbreak of dengue fever in Southeast Asia is "exploding" amid the coronavirus fight*. CNBC. https://www.cnbc.com/2020/07/10/outbreak-of-dengue-fever-in-southeast-asia-is-exploding-amid-the-coronavirus-fight.html.

35. World Health Organization, Special Programme for Research, Training in Tropical Diseases, World Health Organization. Department of Control of Neglected Tropical Diseases, World Health Organization. Epidemic, & Pandemic Alert. (2009). *Dengue: Guidelines for diagnosis, treatment, prevention and control* (new ed.). World Health Organization.

36. Harapan, H., Michie, A., Mudatsir, M., Sasmono, R. T., & Imrie, A. (2019). Epidemiology of dengue hemorrhagic fever in Indonesia: Analysis of five decades data from the National Disease Surveillance. *BMC Research Notes, 12*. https://doi.org/10.1186/s13104-019-4379-9.

37. Suwantika, A. A., Kautsar, A. P., Supadmi, W., Zakiyah, N., Abdulah, R., Ali, M., & Postma, M. J. (2020). Cost-effectiveness of dengue vaccination in Indonesia: Considering integrated programs with *Wolbachia*-infected mosquitos and health education. *International Journal of Environmental Research and Public Health, 17*(12). https://doi.org/10.3390/ijerph17124217.

38. Rothman, A. L. (2011). Immunity to dengue virus: A tale of original antigenic sin and tropical cytokine storms. *Nature Reviews Immunology*, *11*(8), 532–543. https://doi.org/10.1038/nri3014.

39. Halstead, S. B. (2014). Dengue antibody-dependent enhancement: Knowns and unknowns. *Microbiology Spectrum*, *2*(6), 2.6.30. https://doi.org/10.1128/microbiolspec.AID-0022-2014.

40. Saint Louis University (2015, December). *World's first dengue vaccine originated from SLU research.* [Press release]. https://www.slu.edu/news/2015/december/dengue-vaccine.php.

41. Thomas, S. J., & Yoon, I.-K. (2019). A review of Dengvaxia®: Development to deployment. *Human Vaccines & Immunotherapeutics*, *15*(10), 2295–2314. https://doi.org/10.1080/21645515.2019.1658503.

42. Spiegel, J., Bennett, S., Hattersley, L., Hayden, M. H., Kittayapong, P., Nalim, S., . . . & Gubler, D. (2005). Barriers and bridges to prevention and control of dengue: The need for a socio-ecological approach. *EcoHealth*, *2*, 273–290. https://doi.org/10.1007/s10393-005-8388-x.

43. Tapia-Conyer, R., Betancourt-Cravioto, M., & Méndez-Galván, J. (2012). Dengue: An escalating public health problem in Latin America. *Paediatrics and International Child Health*, *32*(Suppl. 1), 14–17. https://doi.org/10.1179/2046904712Z.00000000046.

44. Gubler, D. J. (2011). Dengue, urbanization and globalization: The unholy trinity of the 21st century. *Tropical Medicine and Health*, *39*(4 Suppl.), 3–11. https://doi.org/10.2149/tmh.2011-S05.

45. Sulistyawati, S., Dwi Astuti, F., Rahmah Umniyati, S., Tunggul Satoto, T. B., Lazuardi, L., Nilsson, M., Rocklov, J., Andersson, C., & Holmner, Å. (2019). Dengue vector control through community empowerment: Lessons learned from a community-based study in Yogyakarta, Indonesia. *International Journal of Environmental Research and Public Health*, *16*(6), 1013. https://doi.org/10.3390/ijerph16061013.

46. Kusriastuti, R., Suroso, T., Nalim, S., & Kusumadi, W. (2004). "Together picket." Community activities in dengue source reduction in Purwokerto City, Central Java, Indonesia. World Health Organization. *Dengue Bulletin*, *28*, 35–38.

47. Achee, N. L., Gould, F., Perkins, T. A., Reiner, R. C., Jr., Morrison, A. C., Ritchie, S. A., Gubler, D. J., Teyssou, R., & Scott, T. W. (2015). A critical assessment of vector control for dengue prevention. *PLOS*

Neglected Tropical Diseases, 9(5), e0003655. https://doi.org/10.1371/journal .pntd.0003655.

48. World Health Organization. (2012). *Handbook for integrated vector management.* https://apps.who.int/iris/handle/10665/44768.

2. THE BUSINESS FAMILY: THE TAHIJAS

1. Julius Tahija received the Military Order of William from the Netherlands, its highest honor, for his actions as a sergeant during World War II.
2. Tahija, J. (1995). *Horizon beyond* (p. 187). Singapore: Times Books International.
3. Tahija, J. (1998). *An unconventional woman: An extraordinary love story* (p. 192). New York: Viking.
4. Tahija (1995, p. 212).
5. Interview with George Tahija by R. Edward Freeman and Joseph Burton.
6. Tahija (1998, pp. 222–223).
7. Interview with George Tahija.
8. Tahija (1998, pp. 22–36, 47).
9. Tahija (1998, pp. 57–60).
10. Tahija (1995, pp. 36–37).
11. Tahija (1998, pp. 135–140).
12. Tahija (1998, pp. 193–194).
13. Tahija (1995, pp. 102, 136).
14. Interview with Tahija family by Freeman and Burton.
15. *Yayasan* translates to "foundation" in Indonesian.
16. Yayasan Tahija. (n.d.). Yayasan Tahija Profile. Retrieved February 12, 2024, from https://tahija.or.id/profile.
17. Interview with Victorius Munasdi, conducted and translated by Rita Widiadana.
18. Interview with George Tahija.
19. Interview with George Tahija.
20. Interview with Sunny Susanto conducted and translated by Widiadana.
21. Interview with Dr. Shelly Tahija by Freeman and Burton.
22. Interview with George Tahija.
23. Sumilarv is the brand name for the mosquito larvicide used during the project.

24. Tana, S., Umniyati, S., Petzold, M., Kroeger, A., & Sommerfeld, J. (2012). Building and analyzing an innovative community-centered dengue-ecosystem management intervention in Yogyakarta, Indonesia. *Pathogens and Global Health*, *106*(8), 469–478. https://doi.org/10.1179/20 47773212Y.0000000062.

25. Interview with Dr. Sjakon Tahija, George Tahija, and Laurel Tahija by Freeman and Burton.

26. Tana et al. (2012).

27. Tana et al. (2012, p. 471).

28. Freeman, R. E. (2022). *Yayasan Tahija—A Case-E-0427*. Darden Business Publishing.

29. Interview with Anastasius Wahyuhadi, former chief executive officer, Tahija Foundation, conducted and translated by Widiadana.

30. Interview with Titayanto Pieter conducted and translated by Widiadana.

31. Interview with Sjakon Tahija.

3. THE NEW MOSQUITOES

1. Burki, T. (2020). *Wolbachia*, a bacterium fighting on our side. *The Lancet Infectious Diseases*, *20*(6), 662–663. https://doi.org/10.1016/S1473 -3099(20)30384-4.

2. Werren, J. H., Baldo, L., & Clark, M. E. (2008, October). *Wolbachia*: Master manipulators of invertebrate biology. *Nature Reviews Microbiology*, *6*, 742. https://www.nature.com/articles/nrmicro1969.

3. Werren et al. (2008, October).

4. Eliminate Dengue Program was the original name until 2017. For the purposes of clarity and consistency in this book, we will refer to it by its most recent name, World Mosquito Program (WMP).

5. *Why use the fly in research?* (n.d.). Yourgenome. Retrieved February 4, 2021, from https://www.yourgenome.org/facts/why-use-the-fly-in -research#:~:text=Fruit%20fly%20are%20small%20(3,to%20maintain %20in%20the%20laboratory.

6. Frentiu, F. D., Zakir, T., Walker, T., Popovici, J., Pyke, A. T., van den Hurk, A., McGraw, E. A., & O'Neill, S. L. (2014). Limited dengue virus replication in field-collected *Aedes aegypti* mosquitoes infected with

Wolbachia. PLoS Neglected Tropical Diseases, 8(2). https://doi.org/10.1371
/journal.pntd.0002688; Hoffmann, A. A., Montgomery, B. L., Popo-
vici, J., Iturbe-Ormaetxe, I., Johnson, P. H., Muzzi, F., Greenfield, M.,
Durkan, M., Leong, Y. S., Dong, Y., Cook, H., Axford, J., Callahan,
A. G., Kenny, N., Omodei, C., McGraw, E. A., Ryan, P. A., Ritchie,
S. A., Turelli, M., & O'Neill, S. L. (2011). Successful establishment of
Wolbachia in *Aedes* populations to suppress dengue transmission. *Nature,
476*(7361), 454–457. https://doi.org/10.1038/nature10356.

7. World Mosquito Program. (n.d.). *World Mosquito Program—Releasing
hope.* Retrieved March 13, 2024, from https://www.worldmosquitoprogram
.org/en/news-stories/stories/releasing-hope.

8. Duke-NUS Medical School. (n.d.). *Duane J. Gubler bio.* Duke-NUS
Medical School Directory. https://www.duke-nus.edu.sg/directory
/detail/duane-gubler.

9. Interview with Sjakon Tahija, cofounder and chairman of the Board of
Trustees, Tahija Foundation, by R. Edward Freeman and Andrew Sell.

10. University of Oxford. (n.d.). *Defeating dengue with GM mosquitoes.*
Retrieved February 13, 2024, from https://www.ox.ac.uk/research/research
-impact/defeating-dengue-gm-mosquitoes.

11. Interview with Dr. Cameron Simmons, regional director Oceania,
World Mosquito Program Global, by Rita Widiadana.

12. Annual Report Tahija (2022). Retrieved March 14, 2024, from https://
tahija.or.id/myreports-item/annual-report-tahija-2022.

13. Interview with Sjakon Tahija by Freeman and Joseph Burton.

14. Interview with Sjakon Tahija.

15. Interview with Shelly Tahija by Freeman and Burton.

16. Interview with Laurel Tahija by Freeman and Burton.

17. Interview with George Tahija by Freeman and Burton.

18. WMP Yogyakarta and WMP Global are two distinct organizations.
The Yogyakarta organization was funded and managed by the Tahija
Foundation and headquartered in Indonesia. The WMP Global organization was headquartered in Australia and led by Scott O'Neill. It is
often known simply as the World Mosquito Program. A memorandum
of understanding detailed the relationship and structure among the
staff across all partner organizations.

4. THE PARTNERSHIP

1. Wibawa, T. (2020, January 3). *Indonesia and Australia at a "strategic turning point" as relationship reaches 70-year milestone*. ABC News. https://www.abc.net.au/news/2020-01-04/indonesia-australia-reaches-70-years-diplomatic-relations/11825010.

2. Laughland, O., & Anjani, K. (2013, December 5). Indonesia and Australia to set up hotline to contain phone-tapping fallout. *The Guardian*. http://www.theguardian.com/world/2013/dec/05/indonesia-australia-hotline-phone-tapping-nsa.

3. Interview with Anastasius Wahyuhadi, conducted and translated by Rita Widiadana.

4. Universitas Gadjah Mada. (2019, June 14). *History*. https://ugm.ac.id/en/about-us/3683-history.

5. Suryadinata, L. (n.d.) *Gajah Mada: Prime minister of Majapahit Empire. Encyclopaedia Britannica*. Retrieved February 15, 2024, from https://www.britannica.com/biography/Gajah-Mada.

6. Universitas Gadjah Mada. (2021, September 10). *Vision and mission*. Retrieved February 15, 2024, from https://ugm.ac.id/en/about-us/1321-vision.and.mission.

7. Interview with Professor Panut Mulyono, rector, University of Gadjah Mada, conducted and translated by Widiadana; Interview with Dr. Ova Emilia, dean of Faculty of Medicine, Public Health and Nursing, University of Gadjah Mada, conducted and translated by Widiadana; interview with Dr. Ali Ghufron Mukti, former dean of Faculty of Medicine and Public Health, University of Gadjah Mada, conducted and translated by Widiadana.

8. Interview with Wahyuhadi.

9. Interview with Scott O'Neill by Widiadana.

10. Interview with Michael Adrian Widjanarko, legal counsel, Tahija Enterprise, conducted and translated by Widiadana.

11. Interview with Sjakon Tahija by R. Edward Freeman and Joseph Burton.

12. Interview with Laurel Tahija by Freeman and Burton.

13. Interview with Dr. Adi Utarini, faculty member, University of Gadjah Mada, and WMPY principal investigator/project leader, conducted and translated by Widiadana.

14. Interview with Utarini.

15. Interview with Dr. Riris Andono Ahmad conducted and translated by Widiadana.

16. Alvarez, S., & Sachs, S. (2023). Where do stakeholders come from? *Academy of Management Review, 48*(2), 187–202. https://doi.org/10.5465/amr.2019.0077.

17. Interview with Renggoaini Jahya, WMPY knowledge management team leader, conducted and translated by Widiadana.

18. Interview with Widi Nugroho, WMPY general manager, conducted and translated by Widiadana.

19. Interview with Utarini.

5. MORE STAKEHOLDERS

1. Interview with Adi Utarini, faculty member, University of Gadjah Mada, and WMPY principal investigator/project leader, conducted and translated by Rita Widiadana.

2. Interview with Dr. Sofia Mubarika Haryana, deputy dean of the Faculty of Medicine and Public Health, University of Gadjah Mada, conducted and translated by Widiadana.

3. University of Melbourne. (n.d.). *Professor S Yati Soenarto*. Retrieved February 17, 2024, from https://mdhs.unimelb.edu.au/engage/community/awards-and-honours/yati-soenarto.

4. Bines, J. E., At Thobari, J., Satria, C. D., Handley, A., Watts, E., Cowley, D., Nirwati, H., Ackland, J., Standish, J., Justice, F., Byars, G., Lee, K. J., Barnes, G. L., Bachtiar, N. S., Viska Icanervilia, A., Boniface, K., Bogdanovic-Sakran, N., Pavlic, D., Bishop, R. F., . . . & Soenarto, Y. (2018). Human neonatal rotavirus vaccine (RV3-BB) to target rotavirus from birth. *New England Journal of Medicine, 378*(8), 719–730. https://doi.org/10.1056/NEJMoa1706804.

5. Ministry of Health Report 2022, p 132. Retrieved March 13, 2024, from: https://p2p.kemkes.go.id/profil-kesehatan-2022/.

6. Interview with Professor Yatie Soenarto, conducted and translated by Widiadana.

7. Utarini, A. (2016, June 20). *How we convinced people to trust a new innovative approach to eliminate dengue.* The Conversation. http://theconversation.com/how-we-convinced-people-to-trust-a-new-innovative-approach-to-eliminate-dengue-56692.

8. Monfries, J. (2008). The sultan and the revolution. *Bijdragen Tot de Taal-, Land- En Volkenkunde, 164*(2/3), 269–297.

9. Interview with Anastasius Wahyuhadi, former chief executive officer, Tahija Foundation, conducted and translated by Widiadana.

10. Tahija, J. (1995). *Horizon beyond.* Times Books International.

11. Interview with Sri Sultan Hamengkubuwono X, conducted and translated by Widiadana.

12. Interview with Wahyuhadi.

13. Interview with Widi Nugroho, WMPY general manager, conducted and translated by Widiadana.

14. Interview with Sri Sultan Hamengkubuwono X.

15. A multistakeholder partnership is loosely defined as two or more distinct organizations that enter into an agreement for a common purpose regardless of either organization's sector or category.

16. Interview with Victorious Munasdi, WMPY stakeholders liaison officer, conducted and translated by Widiadana.

17. Interview with Munasdi.

18. Interview with Dr. Bambang Setiadi, deputy minister, Indonesian Ministry of Research and Technology, conducted and translated by Widiadana.

6. COMMUNITY

1. Statistics Indonesia. (n.d.). *Number of population results SP2020 by region and gender (people), 2020.* Retrieved March 13, 2024, from https://www .bps.go.id/en/statistics-table/2/MjEzMSMy/number-of-population -results-sp2020-by-region-and-gender.html.

2. Statistics Indonesia. (n.d.). *Percentage of urban population by province, 2010–2035.* Retrieved March 13, 2024, from https://www.neliti.com /publications/51230/percentage-of-urban-population-by-province -2010-2035.

3. Provinsi DI Yogyakarta. (n.d.). *Sensus Penduduk 2010.* Badan Pusat Statistik. Retrieved February 20, 2024, from https://sensus.bps.go.id/main /index/sp2010.

4. Britannica Encyclopaedia editors. (n.d.). Yogyakarta—Indonesia. *Encyclopaedia Britannica.* Retrieved February 20, 2024, from https://www .britannica.com/place/Yogyakarta-Indonesia.

5. Smithsonian Institution. (n.d.). *Global volcanism program: Merapi*. Smithsonian Institution, National Museum of Natural History. Retrieved February 20, 2024, from https://volcano.si.edu/volcano.cfm?vn=263250.

6. Utama, I. M. S., Lukman, N., Sukmawati, D. D., Alisjahbana, B., Alam, A., Murniati, D., . . . & Karyana, M. (2019). Dengue viral infection in Indonesia: Epidemiology, diagnostic challenges, and mutations from an observational cohort study. *PLOS Neglected Tropical Diseases, 13*(10), e0007785. https://doi.org/10.1371/journal.pntd.0007785.

7. Interview with George Tahija by R. Edward Freeman and Joseph Burton.

8. Interview with Victorious Munsadi, conducted and translated by Rita Widiadana.

9. Utarini, A. (2016, June 20). *How we convinced people to trust a new innovative approach to eliminate dengue*. The Conversation. http://theconversation.com/how-we-convinced-people-to-trust-a-new-innovative-approach-to-eliminate-dengue-56692.

10. Interview with Bekti Andari, WMPY community engagement team leader and stakeholders engagement team leader, conducted and translated by Widiadana.

11. Interview with Andari.

12. Tantowijoyo, W., Andari, B., Arguni, E., Budiwati, N., Nurhayati, I., Fitriana, I., Ernesia, I., Daniwijaya, E. W., Supriyati, E., Yusdiana, D. H., Victorius, M., Wardana, D. S., Ardiansyah, H., Ahmad, R. A., Ryan, P. A., Simmons, C. P., Hoffmann, A. A., Rancès, E., Turley, A. P., . . . & O'Neill, S. L. (2020). Stable establishment of *wMel Wolbachia* in *Aedes aegypti* populations in Yogyakarta, Indonesia. *PLOS Neglected Tropical Diseases, 14*(4), e0008157, 4. https://doi.org/10.1371/journal.pntd.0008157.

13. Interview with Victorius D. Munasdi V, WMPY outreach and stakeholder liaison officer, conducted and translated by Widiadana.

14. The first word of each bullet is in the Bahasa Indonesia language. Interview with Nida Budiwati Pramuko, WMPY field entomology team leader, conducted and translated by Widiadana.

15. Interview with Equatori Prabowo, WMPY community and media engagement team leader, conducted and translated by Widiadana.

16. Interview with Andari.

17. Interview with Prabowo.

18. Interviews with Pramuko; Wasini, WMPY field entomology team; and Sigit Setyawan, WMPY field entomology team, conducted and translated by Widiadana.

19. WMPY team member Wasini goes by only one name, as is customary among some Indonesians.

20. Interview with Wasini.

21. The survey designs were based on a two-stage cluster random sampling of Yogyakarta City households and study intervention areas. The survey percentages represent respondents in the intervention areas. The margin of error in the intervention areas was 10 percent.

22. Indriani, C., Tantowijoyo, W., Rancès, E., Andari, B., Prabowo, E., Yusdi, D., Ansari, M. R., Wardana, D. S., Supriyati, E., Nurhayati, I., Ernesia, I., Setyawan, S., Fitriana, I., Arguni, E., Amelia, Y., Ahmad, R. A., Jewell, N. P., Dufault, S. M., Ryan, P. A., . . . & Utarini, A. (2020). Reduced dengue incidence following deployments of *Wolbachia*-infected *Aedes aegypti* in Yogyakarta, Indonesia: A quasi-experimental trial using controlled interrupted time series analysis. *Gates Open Research*, *4*, 50, 5–6. https://doi.org/10.12688/gatesopenres.13122.1.

23. Interview with Ranggoaini Jahya, WMPY knowledge management team leader, conducted and translated by Widiadana.

7. COMMUNITY VOLUNTEERS: WOMEN LEAD THE WAY

1. The World Bank Data. (n.d.). *Labor force participation rate, female (% of female population ages 15+) (modeled ILO estimate)—Indonesia.* International Labour Organisation, ILO Modelled Estimates and Projections database (ILOSTAT). Retrieved February 26, 2024, from https://data .worldbank.org/indicator/SL.TLF.CACT.FE.ZS?locations=ID.

2. Platt, M. (2017). *Marriage, gender and Islam in Indonesia: Women negotiating informal marriage, divorce and desire* (p. 2). Routledge.

3. Rinaldo, R. (2019). Obedience and authority among Muslim couples: Negotiating gendered religious scripts in contemporary Indonesia. *Sociology of Religion*, *80*(3), 323–349. https://doi.org/10.1093/socrel/sry045.

4. Srimulyani, E. (2012). *Women from traditional Islamic educational institutions in Indonesia: Negotiating public spaces* (p. 21). Amsterdam University Press. https://doi.org/10.26530/OAPEN_418531.

5. National Population and Family Planning Board (BKKBN), Statistics Indonesia (BPS), Ministry of Health (Kemenkes), and ICF. (2018). *Indonesia semographic and health survey 2017* (p. xvii). BKKBN, BPS, Kemenkes, and ICF. https://dhsprogram.com/pubs/pdf/FR342/FR342.pdf.

6. BKKBN et al. (2018, pp. 256–269).

7. BBC (2018, May 31). *Sultan of Yogyakarta: A feminist revolution in an ancient kingdom.* https://www.bbc.com/news/world-asia-43806210.

8. Prihatini, E. S. (2020). Retrieved on 14 march, 2024, from https://www.statista.com/statistics/730286/indonesia-proportion-of-seats-held-by-women-in-national-parliament/.

9. Rahman, D. F. (2020, September 2). Female workers in Indonesia earn 23 percent less than their male peers. *The Jakarta Post.* https://www.thejakartapost.com/news/2020/09/20/female-workers-in-indonesia-earn-23-less-than-their-male-peers.html.

10. Centers for Disease Control and Prevention, National Center for Emerging and Zoonotic Infectious Diseases (NCEZID), Division of Vector-Borne Diseases (DVBD). (2021, September 20). *Symptoms and treatment—dengue.* Retrieved February 26, 2024, from https://www.cdc.gov/dengue/symptoms/index.html.

11. Interview with Endah Supriyati, WMPY diagnostic laboratory coordinator, conducted and translated by Rita Widiadana.

12. Interview with Dr. Citra Indriyani, surveillance team leader, University of Gadjah Mada, conducted and translated by Widiadana.

13. Interview with Indah Nurhayati, WMPY mosquito rearing coordinator, conducted and translated by Widiadana.

14. Interview with Anastasia Maya Indah Lestari, WMPY field entomology team member, conducted and translated by Widiadana.

15. Interview with physician Ida Novirawati, Jetis Community Health Center—Yogyakarta, conducted and translated by Widiadana.]

16. Interview with Ryan Wulandari, Pakuncen subdistrict chief, conducted and translated by Widiadana.

17. Anggraini, R. N. E., Rochimah, S., & Soedjono, A. R. (2016). PKK-man: A System to Manage PKK Activities in Indonesia. In *IOP Conference Series: Materials Science and Engineering* (Vol. 105, No. 1, p. 012008). IOP Publishing.

18. Pembinaan Kesejahteraan Keluarga. (PKK). (n.d.). *Pemerintah Desa Jraganan.* Retrieved February 26, 2024, from https://jraganan.desa.id/330-2/;

Adzmy, M. F., & Disyacitta, F. (2018). The Indonesian Family Welfare Guidance Programme (PKK) and the revitalisation of corporatist state organisations: A case study of the mobilisation of support for Dewanti Rumpoko in the 2017 Batu municipal election. *PCD Journal, 6*(1), 1–30. https://doi.org/10.22146/pcd.31291; and World Health Organization (2012). *Sasakawa Health Prize: Stories from South-East Asia.* Regional Office for South-East Asia (pp.53–68).https://apps.who.int/iris/bitstream /handle/10665/205878/B4905.pdf?sequence=1&isAllowed=y.

19. Interview with Basyiruddin, chief of Jomblangan village in Bantul, conducted and translated by Widiadana.

20. SONJO Migunani #8: The Power of Greteh; the Role of PKK in Enforcing Health Protocols. (2021, June 14). *SONJO: Sambatan Jogja.* https://sonjo.id/en/sonjo-migunani-en/the-power-of-greteh-the-role -of-pkk-in-enforcing-health-protocols/.

21. Interviews with PKK volunteers Eti Dwikora, Tari Sudjoko, Titi Nurgiati, and Yuli, conducted and translated by Widiadana.

22. Interviews with PKK volunteers.

23. Interviews with PKK volunteers.

8. THE RESULTS

1. Interview with Heroe Poerwadi, conducted and translated by Rita Widiadana.

2. Indriani, C., Tantowijoyo, W., Rancès, E., Andari, B., Prabowo, E., Yusdi, D., Ansari, M. R., Wardana, D. S., Supriyati, E., Nurhayati, I., Ernesia, I., Setyawan, S., Fitriana, I., Arguni, E., Amelia, Y., Ahmad, R. A., Jewell, N. P., Dufault, S. M., Ryan, P. A., . . . & Utarini, A. (2020). Reduced dengue incidence following deployments of *Wolbachia*-infected *Aedes aegypti* in Yogyakarta, Indonesia: A quasi-experimental trial using controlled interrupted time series analysis. *Gates Open Research, 4*(50), 5. https://doi.org/10.12688/gatesopenres.13122.1.

3. Indriani, C., Tantowijoyo, W., Rancès, E., Andari, B., Prabowo, E., Yusdi, D., Ansari, M. R., Wardana, D. S., Supriyati, E., Nurhayati, I., Ernesia, I., Setyawan, S., Fitriana, I., Arguni, E., Amelia, Y., Ahmad, R. A., Jewell, N. P., Dufault, S. M., Ryan, P. A., . . . & Utarini, A. (2020). Reduced dengue incidence following deployments of *Wolbachia*-infected *Aedes*

aegypti in Yogyakarta, Indonesia: A quasi-experimental trial using controlled interrupted time series analysis. *Gates Open Research*, *4*(50), 10. https://doi.org/10.12688/gatesopenres.13122.1.

4. A secondary analysis was conducted on six additional months of data, through September 2019. It yielded intervention results similar to those obtained in the primary analysis (an estimated 76 percent reduction in dengue cases). This statistic of a 73 percent decline in DHF was based on an interrupted time series analysis with a 95 percent confidence interval between 49 percent and 86 percent. The associated *p*-value was > 0.001.

5. Utarini, A., Indriani, C., Ahmad, R. A., Tantowijoyo, W., Arguni, E., Ansari, M. R., Supriyati, E., Wardana, D. S., Meitika, Y., Ernesia, I., Nurhayati, I., Prabowo, E., Andari, B., Green, B. R., Hodgson, L., Cutcher, Z., Rancès, E., Ryan, P. A., O'Neill, S. L., . . . & Simmons, C. P. (2021). Efficacy of *Wolbachia*-infected mosquito deployments for the control of dengue. *New England Journal of Medicine, 384*(23), 2179. https://doi.org/10.1056/NEJMoa2030243.

6. Utarini et al. (2021, p. 2180). Study investigators had desired to recruit four hundred participants with virologically confirmed dengue (VCD) to achieve a conventional statistical power (80 percent) threshold to detect a 50 percent lower VCD incidence rate between the *Wolbachia* intervention areas and the control areas. Laboratory testing was used to identify VCD participants.

7. Utarini et al. (2021, p. 2177).

8. Interview with Dr. Shelly Tahija by R. Edward Freeman and Andrew Sell.

9. Interview with Dr. Sjakon Tahija by Freeman and Sell.

10. Interview with George Tahija by Freeman and Sell.

11. Interview with Laurel Tahija by Freeman and Sell.

12. Interview with Trihadi Saptoadi, conducted and translated by Widiadana.

13. Interview with Sri Sultan Hamengkubuwono X, conducted and translated by Widiadana.

14. Interview with Berty Murtiningsih, conducted and translated by Widiadana.

15. Interview with Dr. Riris Andono Ahmad, conducted and translated by Widiadana.

16. Interview with Dr. Eggi Arguni, WMPY diagnostic team leader, conducted and translated by Widiadana.

17. Interview with Dr. Warsito Tantowijoyo, WMPY entomology team leader, conducted and translated by Widiadana.

18. Interview with Scott O'Neill, director, World Mosquito Program Global, interviewed by Widiadana.

19. Interview with Dr. Adi Utarini, faculty member, University of Gadjah Mada, WMPY principal investigator and project leader, conducted and translated by Widiadana.

20. Gates, M. F. (2021, September 15). The 100 most influential people of 2021: Adi Utarini. *Time.* https://time.com/collection/100-most-influential -people-2021/6095805/adi-utarini/.

21. AIPI recommendation letter from Satryo Brojonegoro to the Minister of Health of the Republic of Indonesia. (2021, October 7). *Support for the innovation of dengue prevention with* Wolbachia *technology.*

22. Interview with Dr. Claudia Surjadjaja, regional director (Asia), World Mosquito Program Global, conducted and translated by Widiadana.

23. World Mosquito Program. (n.d.). *Impact.* Retrieved February 26, 2024, from https://www.worldmosquitoprogram.org/en/work/wolbachia-method /impact.

24. World Health Organization Vector Control Advisory Group. (2021). *Thirteenth meeting of the WHO Vector Control Advisory Group: Meeting report.* https://www.who.int/publications/i/item/9789240021792.

25. Brady, O. J., Kharisma, D. D., Wilastonegoro, N. N., O'Reilly, K. M., Hendrickx, E., Bastos, L. S., Yakob, L., & Shepard, D. S. (2020). The cost-effectiveness of controlling dengue in Indonesia using *wMel Wolbachia* released at scale: A modelling study. *BMC Medicine, 18*(1), Article 186. https://doi.org/10.1186/s12916-020-01638-2. In the study's cost modeling, societal cost was defined and quantified as "lost wages due to work absences attributable to sickness and the value of life lost due to premature death."

26. Interview with Sjakon Tahija by Freeman and Sell.

9. THE FUTURE

1. Interview with George Tahija by R. Edward Freeman and Joseph Burton.

2. Interview with George Tahija.
3. Interview with Dr. Adi Utarini, faculty member, University of Gadjah Mada, WMPY principal investigator and project leader, conducted and translated by Rita Widiadana.
4. Interview with Trihadi Saptoadi, Tahija Foundation chief executive officer, conducted and translated by Widiadana.
5. Interview with Endah Supriyati, WMPY diagnostic laboratory coordinator, conducted and translated by Widiadana.
6. Interview with Sonny Susanto, Tahija Foundation finance executive, conducted and translated by Widiadana.
7. Interview with Laurel Tahija by Freeman and Burton.
8. Interview with Anastasia Maya Indah Lestari, WMPY community engagement team member, conducted and translated by Widiadana.
9. Interview with Bekti Andari, WMPY community engagement team leader and stakeholders engagement team leader, conducted and translated by Widiadana.

INDEX

₃M Plus, 136, 138

Aedes Aegypti mosquitoes, 12–13, 15, 48, 73, 80, 110, 138, 146, 149

Aedes albopictus, 12–13

Ahmad, Riris Andono, 72, 151, 155

Alphey, Luke, 53

American Society of Tropical Medicine and Hygiene, 43

Andari, Bekti, 101–103, 109, 119, 130, 172, 173

antibody-dependent enhancement of infection, 20

Applying Wolbachia to Eliminate Dengue (AWED) study, 145–146, 148–157

Arguni, Eggi, 122–124, 130, 140, 143, 155

Badan Kependudukan dan Keluarga Berencana Nasional, 126

Bayudono, Ir, 85–86

behavior modification, 22–23

Bill and Melinda Gates Foundation, 51

Bisnis, 116

bottom-up model, 38–39

breakbone fever, 13

business families: and Indonesia, 30; role in societal problems, 164–166. *See also* Tahija family

cluster randomized controlled (CRC) trial, 145

community: development, 27; door to door approach, 111–115; empowerment, 41; engagement process, 171–172; going hyper-local, 105–111; influencers, 115–121; local media, 115–121; national media, 115–121; social media, 115–121; Special Region of Yogyakarta, 95–105

community influencers: local media, 115–121; national media, 115–121; social media, 115–121 community volunteer, 108, 122–143; and community partners, 132–143; overview, 122–124; Tahija family and foundation leadership, 128–129; WMPY project leadership and advisers, 129–132; women's roles in Indonesian society and family life, 124–128

COVID-19 pandemic, 4, 10–11, 158; Indonesia, 17; and PKK, 135; vaccines, 19

Culex pipiens, 47

culture, 33; American, 28; Australian, 28, 54; Chinese, 28; Dutch, 28; Indonesian, 27, 28, 32; Javanese, 128; WMPY team's, 106

cytoplasmic incompatibility (CI), 47–48, 50

dengue fever (DF): death from, 8–9; health consequences of, 13–15; insecticides, 21; outbreak in Yogyakarta, Indonesia, 8; people most at risk, 15–16; strategies to eliminate, 18–25; Tahija family contribution to control of, 1–2; vaccines, 19–20

dengue hemorrhagic fever (DHF), 10–11, 148; health consequences of, 13–15; people most at risk, 15–16

dengue shock syndrome (DSS). *See* dengue hemorrhagic fever (DHF)

dengue virus, 10, 160; history, 10–11; hosts for, 12–13; in Indonesia, 16–18; outbreaks, 11; Southeast Asia, 11; *Wolbachia* bacteria used to fight, 47–52

Dengvaxia® vaccine, 20, 23

Dinas Kesehatan—Daerah Istimewa Yogyakarta, 78

Dwiprahasto, Iwan, 151

Eliminate Dengue Project (EDP) staff, 138

ESG (environmental, social, and corporate governance), 166

Eti, Ibu, 137

Family Welfare Movement *(Pemberdayaan Kesejahteraan Keluarga)*, 108

Fitriana, Iva, 130

Gadjah Mada University. *See* University of Gadjah Mada (UGM)

gender: equality, 127–128, 130; inequality, 128, 130, 168. *See also* women

gotong royong, 135

Gubler, Duane, 17–18, 44, 53, 129; background, 52; and O'Neill, 52

Gusti Kanjeng Ratu Mangkubumi, 126

Hamemayu Hayuning Bawana philosophy, 87

Haryana, Sofia Mubarika, 81–83, 85, 91, 122–124, 130, 140

Hoffmann, Ari, 78
Horizon Beyond (Tahija), 86
human behavior: modification,
22–25; public health campaigns,
22–23
"hyper-local" approach, 2

Ikanisasi, 136
Independent Data Monitoring
Committee (IDMC), 93
Indonesia: and business families,
30; Communist coup in, 30;
COVID-19 pandemic, 17;
dengue virus in, 16–18; field
studies in, 144–145; geography,
16; national health education
programs, 23; revolution
against Dutch rule, 85; Special
Region of Yogyakarta, 95–105;
strategies to eliminate dengue,
18–25
Indonesian Academy of Science
(AIPI), 159
Indonesian archipelago, 64
Indonesian Cancer Foundation, 81
Indonesian Institute of Science
(LIPI), 79
Indonesian society and family life,
124–128; nuclear family, 125;
women roles in, 124–128
Indonesian women, 125, 128, 130. *See
also* women
Indriyani, Citra, 130–131
insecticides, 21, 23, 73
integrated vector management
(IVM) handbook, 24

intellectual property (IP) rights,
66–67
interspecies transmission, 13

Jahja, Ranggoaini, 118, 130
Jakarta Post, The, 116
Javanese culture, 128
Johns Hopkins University, 129
Johnson, Petrina, 78, 131

knowledge management (KM),
118–119
Kompas, 116

laboratory mosquitoes, 46–47
Lestari, Anastasia Maya Indah, 171
local media, 115–121

Majapahit Empire, 64
Marzuki, Sangkot, 79
Mayo Clinic, 14
media: local, 115–121; national,
115–121; social, 115–121
Monash University, 48, 53, 65, 67, 75,
78, 81–82, 93, 122–123, 131
Mukti, Ali Ghufron, 81
multi-stakeholder engagement
(MSE), 88–93
multistakeholder partnerships
(MSPs), 173–176
Munsadi, Victorious, 33, 91, 98
Murtiningsih, Berty, 154
Muslim family law, 125

National Ethical Commission, 83
national media, 115–121

Novirawati, Ida, 133
Nugroho, Widi, 74–75
Nurhayati, Indah, 130–132

O'Neill, Scott, 44, 48–51, 52, 61–62,
    69, 80, 82, 92, 123, 156–157
Orang Kaya Baru (OKB), 123–124

partnership: Australian connection,
    61–62; managing WMPY project
    at foundation, 74–78; working
    together, 67–73; Yogyakarta and
    University of Gadja Mada, 62–67
Pemberantasan Sarang Nyamuk, 136
Pemberdayaan Kesejahteraan
    Keluarga (PKK), 134–139, 175;
    and community members, 139;
    during COVID-19 pandemic,
    135; monthly meetings with
    WMPY staff, 139; women, 139,
    142
"phase-gate process," 76
Pieter, Titayanto, 42
Pramuko, Nida Budiwati, 130
Probowo, Equatory, 110
public health campaigns, 22–23
puskemas/community health centers,
    133

quasi-experimental trial study
    (QET), 145–148

respect, as concept in Indonesia,
    68, 167
Rukun Tetangga, 107
Ryan, Peter, 52–53

Sanofi Pasteur, Inc., 20
Saptoadi, Trihadi, 153, 168, 171, 174
Satu Rumah Satu Jumantik, 136
serotypes, 10, 19–20
Setiadi, Bambang, 92
Simmons, Cameron, 54
social media, 115–121
Soenarto, Yatie, 81–82, 83, 91, 123–124,
    130, 140
stakeholder capitalism, 166, 171–173
"stakeholder inquiry system" (SIS),
    98–100
stakeholders: collegial support,
    80–84; multi-stakeholder
    engagement, 88–93; sultan of
    Yogyakarta, 85–88
Sultan Hamengkubuwono I, 96
Sultan Hamengkubuwono IX, 85, 87
Sultan Hamengkubuwono X, 85,
    97, 154
sultan of Yogyakarta, 85–88
Sumilarv project, 35, 41–42, 44, 52, 55,
    63–64, 67, 81, 129, 136, 170
Supriyati, Endah, 130, 168
Surjadjaja, Claudia, 160
Susanto, Sonny, 33, 169
sweat equity, 57

Tahija, George, 28, 31–33, 98, 152,
    165–166, 169, 175; on Tahija
    Foundation, 34; on Wolbachia
    technique, 58–59
Tahija, Jean, 28–30, 32, 54–55
Tahija, Julius, 26–28, 29–30, 32–33,
    86, 87, 168
Tahija, Laurel, 70, 128–129, 153, 170

Tahija, Shelley, 31, 34, 61, 81, 128–129, 152

Tahija, Sjakon, 30, 31–32, 43, 52, 58, 61, 70, 81, 152

Tahija family: business growth, 31; contribution to control of dengue fever, 1–2; and foundation leadership, 128–129; values champions, 33; values guardians, 33

Tahija Foundation, 4, 24–25, 32, 55, 61, 67, 124; adoption of Indonesian village, 34; failure of water intervention, 37–44; George Tahija on, 34; and intellectual property rights, 66–67; management and staff, 123; organizational values, 107; as philanthropic organization, 173; purpose and values, 167–170; and sultan of Yogyakarta, 85–88; venture philanthropy, 55–57; water treatment intervention, 35–38; worked with PKK, 136

Tantowijoyo, Warsito, 94–95, 104, 107, 119, 121, 155

Tari, Ibu, 138

Trial Steering Committee (TSC), 93

trust, as concept in Indonesia, 28, 33, 68–70, 72, 100–103

University of Gadjah Mada (UGM), 1, 4, 38, 60, 61, 62–67, 70, 123, 129, 158; Ethics Board, 83;

Faculty of Medicine and Public Health, 140; laboratory and insectarium, 124

University of Gothenburg (Sweden), 38

University of Indonesia (UI), 79, 144; Ethics Board, 83

Utarini, Adi, 70–71, 77, 79, 91–92, 130, 143, 151, 156–158, 167, 168, 174

vaccines, 19–20, 54

Vector Control Advisory Group, WHO, 161

venture capital (VC) investors, 56

venture philanthropy (VP), 55–57

virologically confirmed dengue (VCD), 151–152

volunteer. See community volunteer

Wahyuhadi, Anastasius, 41, 63, 85–88

Warsito Tantowijoyo, 45–46, 59–60

WMP Global, 53–54, 61–63, 65, 129, 160, 189n18; effectiveness of Wolbachia technology, 145; and intellectual property rights, 66–67; knowledge management interests/practices, 119; scientists, 72–73; study's cost-effectiveness, 162

WMPY. See World Mosquito Program Yogyakarta

Wolbachia bacteria, 1, 54, 80, 82, 110; AWED study, 148–151; cytoplasmic incompatibility, 50; used to fight dengue virus, 47–52

Wolbachia-infected mosquitoes, 3, 48–49, 61, 77, 81, 83, 88, 94, 103, 117, 146, 148–149, 151–152; Townsville, Australia, 51

Wolbachia technology/techniques, 76, 80, 87, 90, 91, 94–95, 99–100, 102, 118, 120, 122–123, 129, 131, 141, 144–145, 156–162, 165, 175–176

women: association, 134, 135; authority inequalities, 125; educational attainment, 126; employment statistics, 126; empowerment, 126, 127; gender-based household role disparities, 125; generating income for, 125; in government positions, 134; parliamentary representation, 127; as PKK health cadres, 136; as PKK members, 136; power disparity, 124–125; roles in Indonesian society and family life, 124–128; as sultan of Yogyakarta, 127; workforce disparities, 125. *See also* gender

World Bank, 124

World Health Organization (WHO), 9, 24, 38, 161

World Mosquito Program (WMP), 4, 48, 51, 53, 65, 129, 145; challenge, 175; *Wolbachia* technology, 61–62, 65, 81

World Mosquito Program Yogyakarta (WMPY), 4–5, 60, 67, 99, 124, 128, 133–134, 139, 160–161, 189n18; community engagement activities, 140; entomology team, 141; field studies, 133, 140; leadership and advisers, 129–132; lessons learned from, 164; project's goals, 122

World War II, 96

Wulandari, Ryan, 134

Yayasan Tahija. *See* Tahija Foundation

Yogyakarta, Indonesia: dengue fever outbreak, 8; insectarium in, 122; QET study in, 145–148; spiritual leadership in, 126; sultan of, 126; and University of Gadja Mada, 62–67; WMPY studies in, 136; women in, 126; world-class laboratory in, 122

Yudhoyono, Susilo Bambang, 62